HINTS ON THE MANAGEMENT OF HAWKS

A Falcon on the Block.

From a Photograph by Reginald Lodge.

HINTS ON THE

MANAGEMENT OF HAWKS
AND PRACTICAL FALCONRY

Chapters Historical and Descriptive

JAMES EDMUND HARTING

LONDON:
THE TABARD PRESS LIMITED
1970

Second edition published 1898 by Horace Cox, London
This edition published 1970 by The Tabard Press, London

This volume has been reproduced
as a facsimile bearing the
original corrigenda

SBN 90195107 2

Reproduced and Printed in Great Britain by
Redwood Press Limited
Trowbridge & London

Introduction to 1970 Edition

James Edmund Harting wrote a number of articles on Falconry as well as books on Natural History which include 'Ornithology of Shakespeare', 'Essays on Sport and Natural History', 'Recreations of a Naturalist' and the well-known 'Bibliotheca Accipitraria', which is a catalogue of all the books, British and foreign, published up to this time of writing and which has some very interesting notes on the History of Falconry.

Harting learnt his falconry from two very experienced falconers – John Barr and the famous Adrian Mollen, hawk trapper and falconer from Valkenswaard in Holland, hence his considerable competance in writing on the subject.

An added interest to 'Hints on Hawk' lies in the illustrations, drawn by the late G. E. Lodge considered to be one of the finest ever painters of birds of prey.

Naturally, there have been improvements in training methods since Harting's day, for instance, nobody kept a check on the condition of Hawks by weighing them regularly, but in the main, Harting's lucid hints have not been superceded and should be read by all falconers, expert or novice.

It is easy to criticise any Advice on outdoor activities on the grounds that the theory and experience in the book often bear little resemblance to the actual, and in this case it would be well to remember that no two hawks are the same, and that no book on falconry can hope to cover all the foibles of one's own birds. Nevertheless, this is a classic and all falconers should welcome its reappearance as did Harting's contemporaries when it made its debut in 1898.

Philip Glasier
The Falconry Centre, Newent, Gloucestershire.

CONTENTS.

HINTS ON THE MANAGEMENT OF HAWKS.

PRACTICAL FALCONRY.

ILLUSTRATIONS.

FULL PAGE.

IN THE TEXT.

HINTS

ON THE

MANAGEMENT OF HAWKS.

FOR some years past I have been in the habit of receiving from various parts of the country a great many letters asking for information about the management of hawks, from which it may be inferred that an interest in the old sport is being revived, and that there are many who would be glad to take it up, did they know exactly how to set about it. In replying to these inquiries, I have generally referred the readers to the recognised text-books on the subject—Salvin and Brodrick's "Falconry in the British Islands," published by Van Voorst; Freeman and Salvin's "Falconry: its Claims, History, and Practice," published by Longmans; and "Practical Falconry," by "Peregrine," published at the *Field* Office.* To judge by the nature of the questions asked, it would seem that the inquirers experience certain difficulties at

* These books, unfortunately, are now all out of print; but since the first edition of the present work was published a good treatise on Falconry, by the Hon. G. Lascelles, has been issued in the Badminton Library.

starting which the works referred to do not enable them satisfactorily to overcome; not always because the books do not contain the information needed, but because the method of teaching adopted by the authors does not "begin at the beginning," and assume no previous knowledge of the subject on the part of the reader.

Many persons who take up falconry for the first time make the mistake of sending for a hawk before they have made any preparations for keeping it properly, and on its arrival are puzzled to know how to handle it, where to keep it, and how and when to feed it.

Such questions as the following are often asked: "What sort of a cage ought I to keep it in?" "Should the cage be indoors?" "How many times a day ought I to feed the bird?" and "Is it necessary always to give it sparrows or other small birds?"

In replying to these and other questions, which imply that the inquirers have no idea how to start (for to put a hawk in a cage would be to ruin the flight feathers), I will offer a few practical hints which I think will be found useful, and which at least have the recommendation of having been derived from experience.

Choice of a Hawk.

The beginner will have first to consider what kind of hawk he proposes to keep, and this must in a measure depend upon the sort of country he lives in. He may have a Merlin, or a Peregrine, both long-winged hawks, which are trained to the lure; or he may have a Sparrowhawk, or Goshawk, which are short-winged hawks, trained to the fist. Any one of the three first-named may be procured in this country; for the last he will have to send abroad.

One of the most easily procured hawks, of

FIG. 1.—THE KESTREL.

course, is the Kestrel or Windhover, known to keepers in Sussex as the Vanner (*i.e.*, fanner) Hawk. But, although it may be readily tamed and trained to fly to the lure, it is useless for hawking purposes, since neither its courage nor its natural instinct prompts it to take its prey like other falcons; its usual food consisting of beetles, grasshoppers, field mice, and such small birds as it can capture by stealth rather than by direct flight and real stooping.

For a beginner I would certainly recommend a Merlin. No hawk so soon becomes tame, or is more easily trained, and, at the same time, is less liable to be lost. An eyess tiercel, however—that is, a male Peregrine taken from the nest—is almost as tractable, and, if properly handled, will become tame in an incredibly short time, manifesting a docility which, to persons knowing nothing about hawks, is very surprising. Sparrowhawks and Goshawks need rather more skill in handling, requiring to be carried a great deal, and have at first a troublesome habit of "bating off," or flying from the hand, every few minutes, hanging head downwards by the jesses, and requiring to be gently and adroitly replaced with a frequency which is very trying to the patience of the owner. On this account I would say to the tyro, begin with a Merlin, or eyess Peregrine.

Merlins nest on the ground on the moors; Peregrines breed in cliffs or on mountain-sides, and young birds of either species may be obtained without much difficulty, by means of a bow-net snare (to be described further on). The proper time to take them is just after they have left the nest and are full feathered; they should never be taken half fledged from the nest, for if they do not die, as is likely, they never turn out good birds when taken so young, and often grow up confirmed "screamers"—a most disagreeable habit, and difficult to cure.

When choosing a hawk, see that the eyes are full and bright: sunken eyes and contracted pupils are a sure indication of ill-health. The tongue and inside of the mouth should be pink: a furred tongue of a whitey-brown colour is a bad sign. The head should be flat, the shoulders broad, the wings long and well crossed over the tail when closed. The pectoral muscles (under the wing) should be full and firm to the touch, not soft and flabby. The

Fig. 2.—An Eyess Peregrine.

flight feathers should be perfect (ten in each wing), and should have good broad webs. It is easy to examine them after hooding the bird by gently expanding each wing by turn. The thighs should be muscular, the feet large and strong. They may be tested by carrying the hawk hooded against the wind, when you will soon discover if the bird in holding on has a good grip.

Let us suppose, then, that the tyro has decided to have either a Merlin or a Peregrine, it matters little which ; the next thing is to prepare for its reception, so that on its arrival there may be no risk of breaking flight or tail feathers for want of proper accommodation.

The Perch.

If the owner lives in the country and has an out-house to spare, which he can fit up as a hawk-house, so much the better ; if not, he will have to fit up a perch indoors. In any case, the construction of the perch will be the first thing to attend to. It is not necessary that it should be a fixture, but it must be sufficiently steady to resist any movement when an unhooded hawk tied on it bates off, as it will often do, with a vigorous stroke of wing.

The form of perch which I have found in every way suited to ordinary requirements, especially where only a cast of hawks (two) is kept, is that figured opposite. Any carpenter can make it in a day, and it is not expensive. Two upright standards are cut, three feet in height, and two inches thick, neatly bevelled off at the edges, with a head of three and a half inches in width which is bored with a hole $1\frac{1}{4}$in. in diameter to receive the end of the perch, which should fit into it perfectly tight. As it would never do for the perch to turn round in the head of the standard (as a hawk suddenly flying off might cause it to do), it is advisable to get a couple of brass-headed thumb-screws of the shape figured in the cut (A), and drive them through the head of each standard into each end of the perch. The latter can then never slip, the head of the screw becomes useful to hang a hood or glove upon, and, moreover enables the perch to be taken to pieces for transport if required. Each standard is morticed into a flat

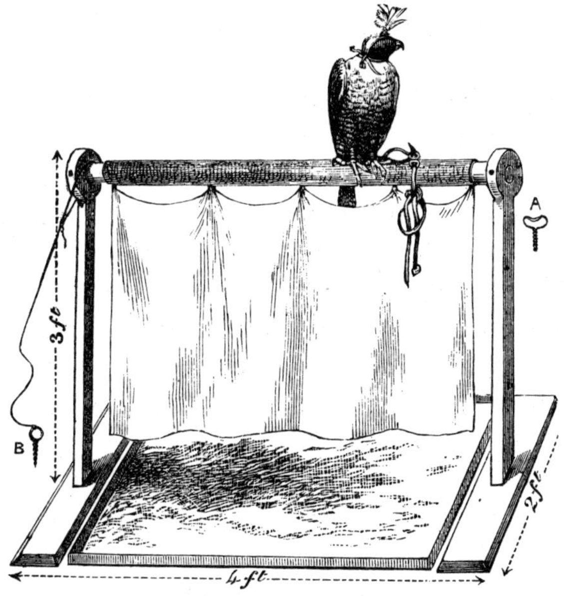

FIG. 3.—THE PERCH.

foot made of 1½in. stuff, 2ft. long and 5½in. wide, bevelled off at the sides and ends.

The horizontal perch, about four feet long, should be slightly greater in diameter than the apertures in the heads of the standards, the ends only being reduced so as to secure a tighter fit. The surface of the perch should be rough, so as to insure a proper foothold for the hawk, which would otherwise experience a difficulty in maintaining its grasp upon a perfectly smooth surface. A piece of maple with the bark on makes a good perch, and has the advantage also of being light; but, as hawks, if kept constantly upon a hard perch or block, are liable to get swollen feet, it is advisable to pad it, and I have found the best material for the purpose to be carpet put on wrong side out. It should be neatly tacked on, care being taken to insert the tacks on the underside of the perch, that is, out of the way of the hawk's feet. The perch is completed by hanging from the under side a curtain about 2ft. 6in. in width, the use of which is to prevent a hawk which has "bated off" from swinging head downwards, which it would do until exhausted, having no power to remount by aid of its beak as a parrot would do. The curtain, which should be weighted at the bottom corners, or tied down, prevents any swing, and the bird with little trouble regains the perch. The material of which this curtain is made may be obtained of any linen-draper, and is technically known as "Hessian" or "wrappering."

To put it on neatly, after hemming the unselvaged sides, a few loops of tape should be sewn on at intervals, and the curtain tacked by these loops to the under side of the perch, leaving open spaces between the loops as shown in the cut. This is necessary in order to admit the fingers when passing the leash through, preparatory to trying a hawk on the perch.

Another point requiring attention is to take care that the swivel is always tied *on the top of the perch*, and sufficiently tight to prevent it from slipping round, in which case the shortness of the jesses would prevent the hawk from getting back to the perch in the event of its "bating off." There is a knack in setting down a hawk gently, upon which a hint may be given. The left hand, upon which the bird is always carried, is rested upon the top of the perch until one end of the leash has been passed over the perch with the right hand, and brought to the front between the perch and the curtain to meet the other end of the leash. Holding the two ends firmly in the right hand, the hawk is lowered just in front of the perch, and pushed gently backwards until both legs touch the perch, when it will step backwards on to it to preserve its balance. The left hand being then disengaged, the leash is tied firmly enough to prevent the swivel from slipping, and the ends are allowed to hang down.

In order to catch the "mutes" or droppings, a zinc tray full of sawdust, or sand, is placed on the floor between the standards, and should exactly fit the space between the feet of the latter. This tray may be 1½in. deep, well soldered at the corners, to make it hold water when used for a bath, of which more anon, and to prevent injury to the wings when the hawk is so using it.

The sawdust, or sand, will absorb all the moisture from the "mutes," and need only be changed every other day. By way of giving additional steadiness to the perch, a brass ring-headed screw (B) may be put down into the floor to the right and left of the standards, to which a cord, looped at one end and thrown over the head of each standard, may then be made fast. The best stuff for this purpose is "blind-cord," which is not too thick, and at the same time very strong. We have now constructed a very efficient perch, which is perfectly steady, light in appearance, and taking up very little space in a room. It is only necessary to add that it should stand far enough away from the wall to prevent the outstretched wings of a hawk from brushing against the wall when the bird turns round upon the perch.

A temporary "dado" of floor-cloth, somewhat higher, and a trifle longer than the perch, should be tacked against the wall behind the perch, to prevent the "mutes" from spoiling the wall paper. The advantage of floor-cloth over other material is that it is easily washed down, and so need never be unsightly.

Thus much for indoor accommodation. Out of doors—and to keep in health, a hawk should be as much as possible in the air—another contrivance is needed.

The Block.

This is simply a solid piece of wood of the shape figured in the annexed cut, with an iron spike at one end to secure steadiness by driving it into the ground. It may be from eight to ten inches in height, and six inches across the top. If made larger than this, it is too heavy to move about. An iron ring, somewhat less in circumference than the block at the point where it encircles it, is then countersunk on the block, and when the leash is fastened to the projecting loop of this ring, the latter slips round and round with every movement of the hawk, thus preventing the leash from getting wound tightly round the block. Some falconers reverse the position of the spike, setting the block on its broader base; but on this plan the base of the block is always getting soiled with the mutes; whereas, in the plan figured, the mutes drop clear of the block into the sand around it, which may be changed from

Fig. 4.—The Block.

time to time, and then all looks clean and neat. The top of the block may be slightly channelled, as shown in the sketch, to let the water run off after rain, the grooves being deeper at the edge of the block than in the centre of it.

A simpler form of block (Fig. 5) may be made by sawing up a larch tree (about 18 inches in circumference) into logs about 8 or 10 inches in length. If these are sent to the nearest forge, the blacksmith will quickly insert a spike at one end and a staple at the other. The latter should be driven down on the top for about two-thirds of its length so as to leave a loop to pass the leash through.

The latest form of block, and that now adopted by the members of the Old Hawking Club, is one designed by Mr. J. T. Studley as shown in Fig. 6. About 4in. in diameter, the upper portion is 4in. in depth. The lower stand, which rests flat upon the ground, is 1½in. in depth. Between the two are a

Fig. 5.—A Simpler Form of Block.

couple of metal rings or "washers," and between these rings is a long loop to project beyond the edge of the block. The iron pin, which is driven into the ground, goes through the rings and iron loop, and into the upper block. This combination is found to answer very well, for a hawk when unhooded and on the ground may move round and round the block without ever getting hung up, and the leash, being then in a straight line parallel to the ground, instead of coming at an angle from the top of the block (as in the old pattern), the risk of injury to the tail feathers is reduced to a minimum.

During the day (if not wet or windy) the hawk will be out on the block, and at night indoors on the perch.

Birds on their blocks should be hooded as little as possible, only, in fact, when they unduly bate.

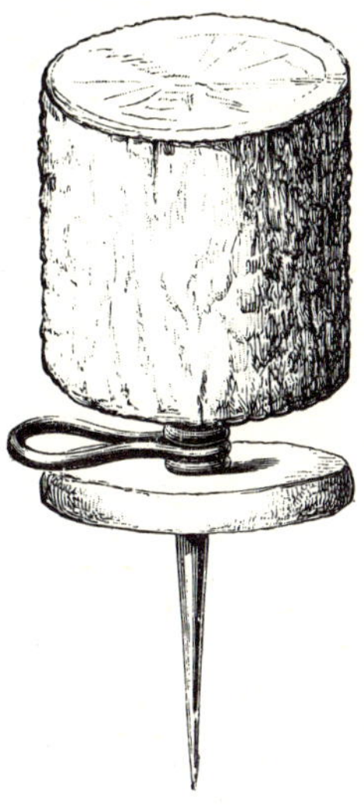

FIG. 6.—STUDLEY'S PATENT BLOCK.

The Rev. G. E. Freeman is of opinion that at night they will do best if placed in a large loft on blocks, with straw on the floor, instead of on a pole.*

The late Lord Lilford pursued an intermediate plan by putting his hawks on a perch so near the

* The *Field*, 26th May, 1894.

floor that if they bated off they came at once to the ground, and could get back easily.

The Bath.

The bath should be given (about twice a week) at the block, and should be put down and filled *before* the hawk is carried out, so as not to alarm the bird unnecessarily. The zinc tray described (p. 9) makes a capital bath, as it is wide and not too deep; and a hawk will go freely into it, stooping down, extending the wings and tail, and throwing the water up over the back like a duck, in evident enjoyment.

Glove, Hood, and Jesses.

Having thus got the perch, block, and bath ready, the next thing is to procure a glove for the left hand (made of buckskin or sheepskin, and having a gauntlet to it), and to order some hoods, jesses, leashes, and swivels. Some falconers make their own hoods, but beginners will want patterns, and, as these are no longer to be bought in England, they will have to send to Holland for them, where they may be procured, together with leashes, swivels, &c., at trifling cost, from Mr. Karl Mollen, Valkenswaard, by Eindhoven, Holland; or from M. Penat, 87, Rue des Petits Champs, Paris. It should be remembered that not only do different hawks require different-sized hoods, but different sizes are needed for the two sexes of the same species. It will be well, therefore, to order some of each.

By some falconers Indian hoods are preferred to Dutch ones. They are cut out of a single piece of leather, and directions for making them, with patterns of the right size for different kinds of hawks will be found in the *Field* of March 15, 1890.

Gloves, of course, may be made to order here, and an old cavalry gauntlet, with the pipeclay beaten

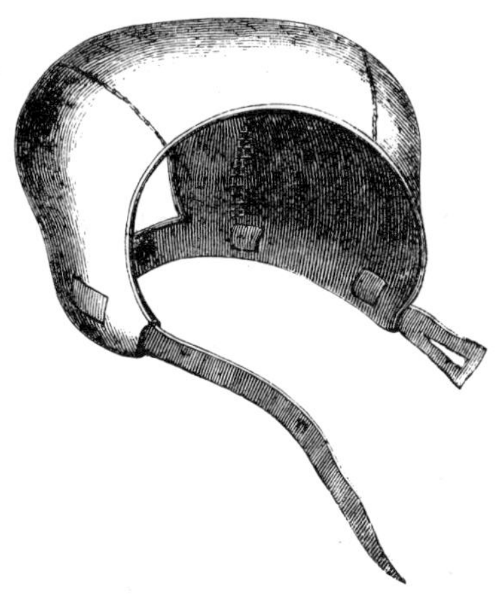

Fig. 7.—A Ruster Hood.

out of it, and dyed brown, will answer the purpose well enough until a glove of more approved make can be procured. A .proper hawking glove may be obtained at a cost of 5*s.* 6*d.* from Mr. Sandell, glover and gaiter maker, Amesbury, Wilts; or may be ordered of any pattern preferred from Mr. Sleep, glover, Knightsbridge. A tracing of the left hand on paper should accompany the order to ensure a proper fit, and care should be taken not to have the glove too tight at the wrist, so that it may pull on and off easily.

When all these preliminaries have been arranged, then, *and not until then*, should the beginner send for a hawk.

Sending a Hawk by Rail.

Having described the preparations which it is necessary to make for the reception of a hawk before sending for it, in order to insure proper treatment on its arrival, I will now suppose that all is in readiness as advised, and that a hawk has been ordered—either a young Peregrine from the cliffs, or a Merlin from the moors, the former costing from 1*l.* to 30*s.*, the latter from 10*s.* to 15*s.*

The sender should be asked to procure a large hamper, and should be furnished with two or three yards of the material called "Hessian" or "wrappering" (already referred to in the description of the perch), with which to line the basket. It should be sewn in all round the inside, *not covering the bottom*, and the inside of the lid should also be lined. This will prevent risk of breaking the flight feathers, and will also prevent injury to the head and eyes, which might otherwise be caused by the bird jumping violently against the lid in its efforts to escape. Matters should be so arranged between the sender and the receiver that the bird should not remain longer in the hamper than can be avoided, and, in the event of a long railway journey being necessary, it should be well fed, without "casting," just before starting. It is better not to put any straw or other material at the bottom of the basket, for, in the event of a sudden jerk, the bird, clutching the straw only, would be thrown violently to one side. It is preferable to allow it to grasp the osier twigs of which the bottom is made.

If the sender has already had some experience of hawks, and can send up a bird with the jesses on and hooded, so much the better; as it will then not only remain perfectly quiet when travelling, and so incur less risk of injury, but will give far less trouble on arriving at its destination. If this cannot be arranged, then the recipient of the bird must manage for himself, and should proceed as follows:

Treatment on Arrival.

Putting on a falconer's glove (always worn on the left hand), open the hamper cautiously, and, taking the hawk gently, yet firmly, by both legs, lift it out clear of the basket as quickly as possible to avoid damage to the wings, which are sure to be outstretched immediately. If the bird has arrived hooded, and with jesses on, it may be set down at once on the perch, the swivel being attached by one end to the jesses, and the leash being put through the other end of the swivel (twice, to prevent its slipping), and then tied firmly to the perch. If, on the other hand, the hawk has only just been caught, and sent up by an inexperienced hand, the first thing to be done on taking it by the legs is to hood it; and care must, of course, be taken to select a hood of the proper size—neither too large, nor too small.

Hooding.

To hood a hawk neatly is a knack which can only be acquired by practice. It requires a light hand, and a certain amount of dexterity in watching the bird, and availing oneself of the right moment when its head is turned in the proper direction—namely, looking towards the falconer's right shoulder. It is useless to try and hood it when looking in the contrary direction, for the beak then will not pass freely through the small opening in front of the hood, but will strike against one side of it, and perhaps jerk the hood out of the falconer's hand.

Repeated clumsy attempts at hooding will do more harm than good, and will only result in making a hawk "hood shy."

There are two or three ways of hooding. Some falconers conceal the hood in the palm of the right hand, holding the plume close up between the thumb and fore finger; and then, touching the hawk's feet with the middle finger to make it look down, pass the back of the hand slowly up the breast until the fingers nearly touch the beak, and then, by a quick turn of the wrist, pop the hood on, pressing the middle finger gently against the back of the head, to help the beak through the front opening.

Others extend the right arm, bringing the hand

slowly round in a semi-circle, and allowing the hawk to watch the approaching hood until it is near enough to be popped quickly on. A third method is to take the hood by the plume with the tips of the thumb and forefinger, and holding it with the opening for the beak downward, stroke the breast feathers gently, getting the hood higher each time, until the

FIG. 8.—THE HOOD PROPER (seen from behind, and open).

"chin strap," as we may term it, is just under the beak, when the sudden elevation of the plume will tilt the hood over the head. John Barr always hooded a hawk in the manner first described, and seldom made a mistake over it; but the second method is, perhaps, more generally adopted, and I think, on principle, is more to be recommended, since it is better to let the hawk see the hood and get accustomed to it, than to run the risk of making a mistake and frightening the bird with a sudden and unexpected movement. The third method I have found very successful with young Peregrines, which may be taught to take their food through the opening of the hood while the latter remains in the falconer's hand. They thus lose all fear of it, and as they draw a mouthful through the opening, the hood may be tilted gently over the head without causing any alarm.

These methods of hooding apply to all hawks, except those which have just arrived unhooded in a hamper. In such a case the only plan is, as I have said, to seize the bird gently and firmly by the legs with the left hand, and so prevent it from evading the hood, which may then be advanced gently towards it, and put on without much difficulty.

It sometimes happens that a hawk after the jesses have been put on, and the hood removed, is so averse to being rehooded that it will fly off the hand every time an attempt is made with that object. In this case it must be hooded while hanging by the jesses head downwards. It only remains to add (for the benefit of the beginner) that as the left hand is occupied with the bird, the mode of fastening a hood is so contrived that it is accomplished with the right hand and the teeth, the left hand being brought forward across the body and lowered, so that the top of the hood is about level with the falconer's chin, the fastentings or "braces" are then easily drawn by the teeth and the right hand. Should a hawk prove troublesome to hood, and jump the moment the hood is put on, thereby throwing it off before it can be braced, the difficulty may be got over as follows:

The hood should be only about half open when it is put on. The moment it is over the head, the end of the brace should be held between the thumb and middle finger, while the forefinger is pressed against the side of the hood. The effect of this will be to close the hood sufficiently to prevent it from falling off should the hawk hang head downwards, and on its regaining the fist, the brace *on the other side* may be drawn with the teeth as above described.

Putting on the Jesses.

After hooding a newly-arrived hawk the next step is to put on the "jesses" (or leg-straps), and, although this is generally done with the help of an assistant to hold the bird (with its wings pressed close against its sides), it may be accomplished unaided as follows: After hooding, and before letting go the legs, pass the leash round the left leg of the bird, and tie it once, bring both ends down between the thumb and forefinger of the left hand, which may then be opened, and the bird allowed to mount and grasp the glove in the position in which a hawk is always carried, that is, facing its owner. Here, owing to the movement of the hand, it will keep restlessly shifting its position, and perhaps try to clutch at the hood in an attempt to pull it off. It must now be transferred to the perch, which is done by lowering the bird backwards against it until the legs touch the perch, when (the ends of the leash being slacked) the bird will step backwards on to the perch, and remain quieter there than on the hand. Tying the leash on temporarily, both hands will now be free to put on the jesses properly: but this must be done very gently, for if any undue restraint be put upon either foot, the bird will at once struggle to free itself, and will attempt to fly off the perch, in doing which it will come down head first. In this case the leash must be at once untied, and the hawk taken up on the glove again, to be retransferred to the perch.

The "jesses" (French *les jets,* from *jeter*, to cast off) are two supple leather straps of the shape, and for a Peregrine tiercel of the size of that shown in the annexed engraving (Fig. 9), one of which is fastened round each leg just above the foot. When once put on they are never removed, except when from wear and tear they require to be renewed. They are left on when a hawk is flown to enable the owner to take up the bird after a flight and hold it on the glove. To put these on, place the hawk's leg midway between the slits A and B; draw the point A through the slit B until the two slits come together and daylight can be seen through *both;* then pass the point C through *both*, and draw up tight. The jess will then be so firmly put on that it will be impossible for the hawk to undo it as it would a knot (see Fig. 16). With one on each leg the ends C hang down. Bring these

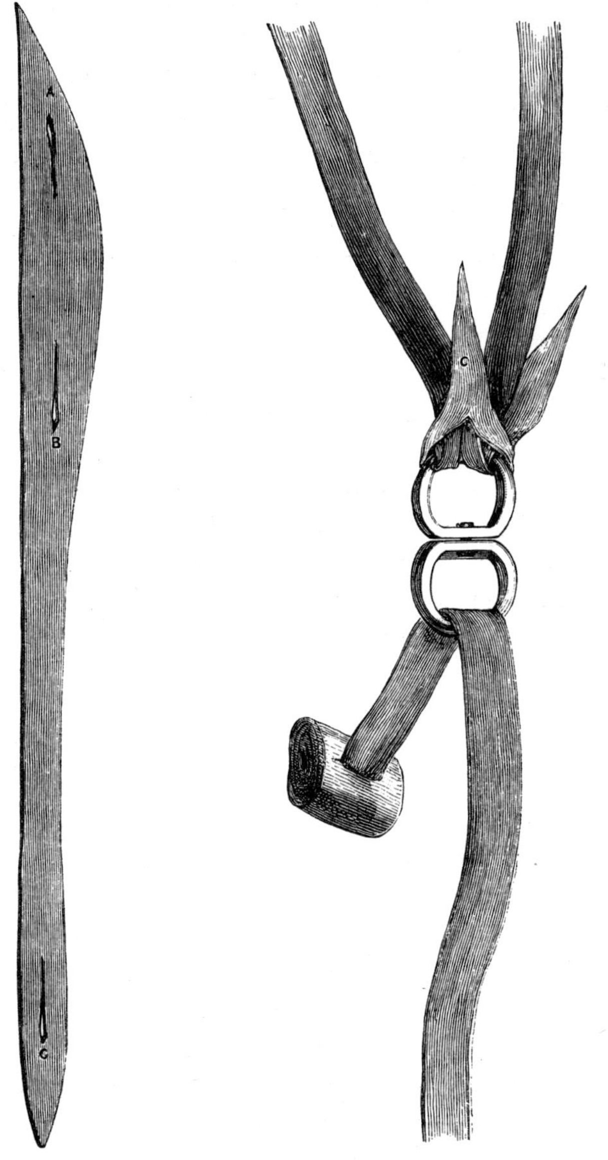

FIG. 9—JESSES, SWIVEL, AND LEASH.

ends together and fasten them on a figure 8 brass swivel, as shown in the cut (Fig. 9). This is effected by putting the end of the jess (C) through one ring of the swivel, and then the swivel through the slit C. The same with the other jess. Through the *other* ring of the swivel is passed the "leash," a narrow leather thong about a yard or so long, one end of which is rolled up to form a "button" too large to pass through the ring of the swivel, the other end being held in the hand when the hawk is carried.

If you have not got a figure 8 swivel, put the leash through the ends of the jesses (C) without it; and by passing it through *twice* you will prevent it from slipping. But if a hawk is tied up in this way temporarily from necessity, it should be looked at from time to time, to see that it does not get hung up with the jesses twisted round its legs.

Varvels.

It was formerly the practice to use "varvels" instead of a swivel, and some falconers still prefer them for a goshawk. These are little flattened silver rings of the diameter of a threepenny piece, which are sewn on, one at the end of each jess. They have this to recommend them, that they need not be removed, as a swivel must be, when the hawk is flown; the leash is easily slipped through them; and, being flat, the owner's name may be engraved on one side, his address on the other, which is useful in case a hawk gets lost. On the other hand, if a hawk be tied on the perch with varvels on, it is apt to get the jesses twisted up tightly in turning round and round, whereas a swivel prevents this.

The Leash.

It is most important to have a good sound leash, cut from a piece of leather of even thickness throughout and without a flaw. It should be about 40 inches in length and half an inch wide, tapering to $\frac{1}{4}$in. within a few inches of the extremity. The "button" at the other end (see p. 23) is formed by tightly rolling the end up two or three times, then making a hole through the centre of the lump thus formed, passing the pointed end of the leash through, and drawing it up as tightly as possible. Without being too large and unsightly, it must nevertheless be always large enough to prevent its being pulled through the ring of the swivel, as I once saw happen when a goshawk "bated" suddenly off her block. The result of this accident was that she went away with the swivel on the ends of her jesses, and we were much afraid she would get hung up in some tree, but having found her after a long search, we got her down with a live hen from the nearest farmyard, tethered to the end of a lure string.

It is by such accidents as these that a falconer learns wisdom.

There is a right and a wrong way of tying the leash to the ring of the block, and one of the first things to be learnt is how to make the *falconer's knot*. It is easier to show how to make it than to describe it; but with the aid of an illustration (Fig. 10), perhaps the following explanation will suffice:—Holding the hawk hooded on the left hand, preparatory to setting her down on the block, with the right hand pass the end of the leash through the ring of the block; then, taking the end between the

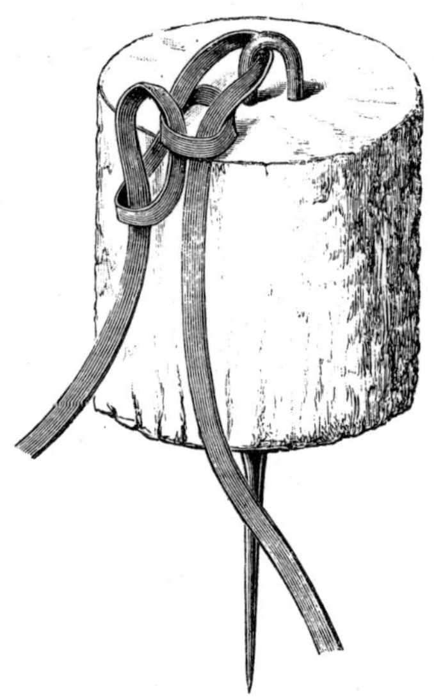

FIG. 10.—THE FALCONER'S KNOT.

forefinger and middle finger, and holding it fairly tight a short distance from the ring (or staple, as the case may be), put the thumb under it (about halfway between the forefinger and the ring), and lift it up and across that portion of the leash, which is between the ring and the *left* hand. It will be seen that a loop is thus made by the thumb. Through this loop the middle finger must guide the end of the leash so as to form another loop, and when this is drawn fairly tight the end is finally passed through this second loop and then hangs down. This knot is, in fact, a slip knot, with the end passed through the loop to *prevent* its slipping. The moment the end is drawn out and pulled sharply, the slip knot gives way, and the hawk is released from the block. It is hardly necessary, perhaps, to say that when setting down a hawk or taking her up from the block, she should be held firmly by the jesses on the left hand until the knot is tied, or untied, as the case may be.

The Brail.

If a hawk during the process of training is troublesome to carry, and frequently bates off the fist, a "brail" should be put on the right wing, that is, the wing nearest the falconer as the bird sits on his left hand. This is a narrow strip of soft leather (about half the width of a jess), having a slit in it about a third of the way down long enough to admit the shoulder of the wing, which being inserted, the longer end is brought down and under the closed wing, and then tied to the shorter end in a bow on the back. This plan effectually prevents a bird from extending its wing, and so "bating off," and for this reason is often adopted when hawks are carried on a cadge in the field, or when travelling. But as a rule only Peregrines and Jerfalcons are thus treated.

A very old plan to make a restless hawk sit quiet

while being carried, and one still practised by the Dutch falconers, is to fill the mouth with cold water, and spurt it over the bird at intervals. This causes the feathers, by a sudden muscular contraction, to be pressed close to the body, and the bird then remains still for some little time.

After being tied on the perch, on which it can readily move about to the extent of its tether, the hawk, if it has travelled in a hood, may now have it removed, the room being previously darkened by drawing down the window blind. But if the bird has arrived unhooded, it should now be left hooded and undisturbed until it is time to feed it. Then will commence the first trial of the falconer's skill and patience.

Feeding.

Hawks vary as much in their tempers and dispositions as do human beings, and accordingly some give very much more trouble at starting than others. I have had some that would feed on the glove unhooded the first night of their arrival; others that would not look at the meat, or remain on the hand for a minute without "bating off." With a troublesome bird of this kind it is well (in order to insure its having a meal) to tie a piece of meat (not too large) on the perch with a bit of twine, before taking off the hood, and leave the room for an hour or so, when the bird, after staring about for awhile and flying off the perch a few times, will at length examine the meat and begin to feed.

For a Peregrine the meat should be fresh lean beef, for a Merlin sheep's heart. The latter is more easily digested, and is the nearest approach in the shape of butcher's meat to the natural food, namely, the flesh of birds. It will not do, however, to feed them on this daily without a change. About every

FIG. 11.—A HOODED HAWK.

third day a Peregrine should have a pigeon, the leg of a fowl, a bit of rabbit with some of the fur on, or a fowl's head and neck, and a Merlin should have a small bird or a mouse or two. This is necessary to keep them in health, for the habit of ejecting through the mouth the indigestible portions of the food enveloped in fur or feathers in the shape of an oval pellet (called by falconers a "casting") is a process natural to them in their wild state, and therefore to be promoted when in captivity. Hawks that are fed in this way are invariably in better health than those fed only on butcher's meat; and a falconer will learn by experience to judge of the health of his birds by the appearance of their "castings." A very important point to be attended to *in hot weather* is never to give meat that is in the least degree tainted, and *in cold weather* to take the chill off the meat by cutting it across and across, and then holding it for a minute or two in the warm hand or before the fire; it must not be dipped in hot water. The meat, if given cold in winter, will cause hawks to shiver, and is very bad for them.

Merlins, to be kept in good condition, should be fed twice a day, about seven in the morning, and about five or six in the evening. The early meal, if light, will not interfere with their flying (when trained) in the afternoon an hour or so before the evening meal. But a Peregrine need only be fed once a day, and that about five o'clock, unless it be an eyess (*i.e.*, a young bird taken from the eyrie, or nest), in which case it should be fed twice a day, like a Merlin, or even oftener, in small quantities, for young and growing hawks require to be very well fed to maintain and increase their strength. Indeed, if they are not thus fed and cared for, they will not only fall off in condition and lose weight, but will exhibit "hunger-traces," as they are called; that is, the feathers of the wing and tail will present the appearance of having sharp cuts across their webs, thereby weakening them and causing them to break off there. The falconer will soon learn to judge of the proper quantity of meat to be given at a meal, by watching the gradual filling and distension of the crop. A Peregrine will generally take about 7oz. or 8oz. at a time, a Merlin of course much less.

It should be borne in mind that a hawk is made tame by the use of the hood, and by being fed always on the glove, or on the lure while held in the hand. Except in the case of birds already trained, it is a mistake to throw down the meat to it as you would throw a bone to a dog. Approach the hawk on the perch very gently with the meat in the gloved hand; let it learn to pull at it, and gradually it will step off the perch on to the glove and continue feeding. The leash must then be untied and the hawk freed from the perch. Or the food may be presented on the lure, to the sight of which the bird will soon get accustomed, and will learn to regard it as the sign of an approaching meal. This is the secret of training. The bird is flown fasting, and comes back to the lure (see p. 35) to be fed.

Washed Meat.

Washed meat is a subject on which a great deal was said and written formerly, but of which one hears but little nowadays, for the simple reason that modern falconers do not much rely on it. Not only do they object to it for eyesses, like Adam Woodcock, the falconer of Avenel in the famous passage by Sir Walter Scott,* but even for rook-hawks, for which it is now only resorted to when a hawk has got "a bit above herself." The effect of "washing" meat, or soaking it in water for a while, and squeezing it dry before it is eaten, is to take a great deal of the nutriment out of it, and to make the hawk more hungry, and therefore more obedient. It was long supposed that it also made them more keen to fly at a quarry such as rooks, of which they do not much like the taste, because the pleasure of feeding on warm, fresh killed flesh would be so great by comparison with their ordinary tasteless food. Modern experience does not altogether justify this idea, but it is not to be rashly admitted that the old authorities were wrong, or that we are right in making so little use of washed meat as we do now.

The late John Barr was a greata dvocate for giving hawks "washed meat" when in training, to make them keen, or, in other words, to create a craving for warm blood. He would not feed them the day they were flown, and their last meal on the previous day would be seven or eight ounces of washed lean beef. To prepare this, it is only necessary to put the beef in cold water for a short time, and squeeze the greater part of the blood out of it. Merlins, as already stated, require a very different treatment.

---

* "The Abbot," ch. iv.

Rangle.

It is a good plan to scatter round the base of the block, occasionally, some small rounded pebbles of the size of beans, and let the birds pick them up, as they will do. I have seen a tiercel on the block pick up seven or eight of such pebbles one after the other in an afternoon, and have watched him throw them up early the next morning on the sawdust below the perch. The old falconers used to give these stones ("rangle" they termed it) the day before flying, either forcing them down the bird's throat as she sat on the perch, or tempting her to swallow them one after another concealed in small pieces of meat. John Barr, from whom I learnt a great deal, always did this, and asserted that it had a beneficial effect in cleansing the crop and panel. It is always better, however, to let the birds pick them up voluntarily, if they will, while sitting on their blocks.

Tiring.

When a hawk, on being fed on the glove or lure, has taken about half a crop full, it is an excellent plan to set her on the perch, or block, and give her a "tiring," that is, a leg or wing of a fowl to pull at, or "tire on," as the old falconers called it. It prevents them from eating too fast, strengthens the muscles of the neck, back, and legs in pulling at the tough parts, and provides them with "casting" in the shape of feathers, which are unavoidably swallowed with almost every mouthful. The more "tiring" a hawk can get the better she will be for it.

Castings.

The state of a bird's stomach and its general condition of health may be judged of by the shape and appearance of the "castings" or pellets, which are thrown up generally early in the morning, and which consist of the fur, feathers, and other indigestible portions of the previous day's meal. If these pellets are oval, firm, and clean, all goes well; but if mis-shapen and covered with mucus, the bird is clearly out of sorts, and after a slight purge of powdered rhubarb, given in a bit of meat, should be kept quiet and warm, and fed on light nourishing meat, such as small birds or rabbit, until an improved appearance of the "castings" indicates a return to health.*

The "casting" should be looked for every morning under the perch, and a hawk should never be flown until some hours after she has got rid of it.

With hawks that are fed twice a day, like Merlins, care should be taken never to give a "casting" at the morning meal, and only half the usual quantity of meat.

---

* The "mutes" also indicate the condition of health. They should be thick chalky-white, with black centre; if thin and watery and of a yellowish or greenish cast, the bird is ailing.

The Lure.

The best lure for a Peregrine is a dead pigeon tied to a string, and the falconer should never go hawking without it. He can never tell when he may require it. He may cast off a tiercel over a field of roots, expecting to find birds, but may beat the entire field while the hawk is "waiting on," and fail to find them, in which case he will have to lure the hawk down, and move on elsewhere. Or, the partridges may be found, flushed and flown at, but may "put in" to some copse or thick covert, from which they cannot easily be dislodged in time to serve the hawk, which must then be taken down.

To go out without a lure might perhaps involve the loss of a hawk. One day, many years ago, I was out rook hawking in Cambridgeshire with Mr. Evans, of Sawston, with whom John Barr had taken service after leaving me. We had some nice passage hawks, which Mr. Evans had got from Holland, and which Barr had trained. They were flying well, but rooks that year were not very plentiful, and we had many a long slip without a kill. On the particular occasion referred to, strange as it may appear, not one of us had a lure! Each thought the other would be sure to have one, and when, after an unsuccessful flight. we had to take a hawk down, there was general consternation when it was found that no one had a lure. What was to be done? The hawk would go away down wind, and perhaps be lost.

" Necessity," they say, " is the mother of invention." Picking up a good sized stone, and knotting it up in my pocket handkerchief, I waited until the hawk was heading towards me, and then flung it up. She came to it at once, and before she had time to discover the deception, I was kneeling down by her

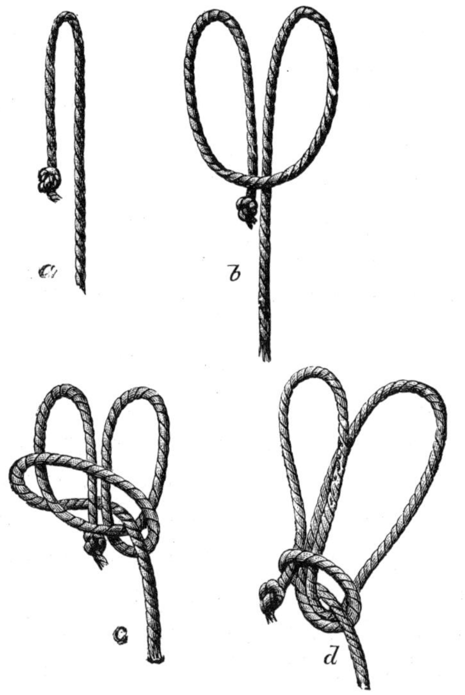

FIG. 12.—FALSE JESSES.

with a good bit of beef in my glove, on to which she soon stepped, and so was taken up. I shall never forget the astonishment of my host, who had never seen this " dodge " put in practice before, although Barr, of course, knew all about it.

While on the subject of lures, it will be well to show the proper way of putting a dead pigeon on a string. A pair of "false jesses," as one may term them, are made at the end of the lure string. The

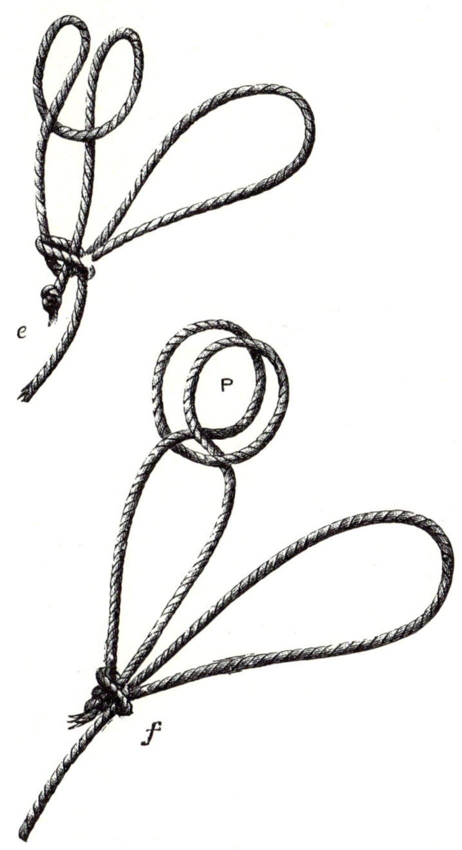

FIG. 13.—FALSE JESSES.

accompanying figures (12 and 13 *a—f*) show the different stages of the knot, and the last of them (13 *f*) shows where one leg of the pigeon (P) has to be inserted, the other leg, of course, being inserted in the corresponding half of the jess, on which a similar clove hitch is made. In this way a useful appliance is very easily and quickly made.

But pigeons are not always to be obtained when wanted, and it is just as well to have by you, ready for use, a more artificial, but sufficiently serviceable form of lure, which may be made as follows: Get a

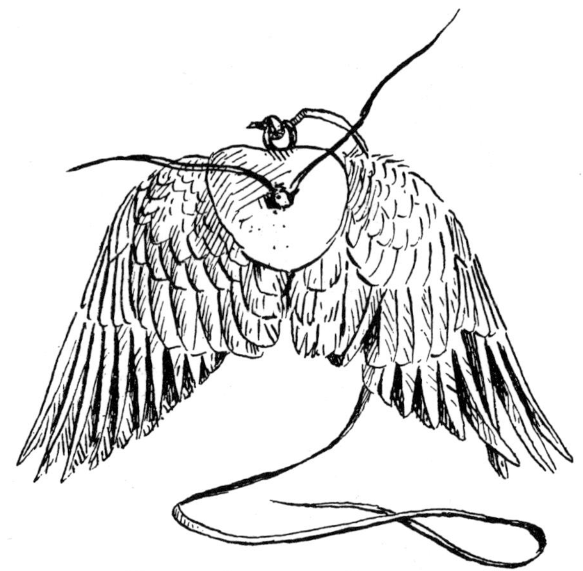

FIG. 14.—LURE FOR A PEREGRINE.

couple of pigeon's wings, tie the wing bones securely together, but two or three inches apart, and in the space between them place a piece of lead, the size and shape of a crown piece, with a hole drilled in it. Cover this well with leather, and stitch the edge of the leather all round right through each wing, so as to form, as it were, a covered platform between the half-extended wings (Fig. 14). A lure-string may then be passed through the hole in the lead by which to swing it, and a lace through each side of the leather will serve to tie on the meat with which it is to be garnished. It is weighted to enable it to be swung and thrown up in the air, but need not be too heavy, lest when a hawk is being "flown to the lure" for exercise, she should, in her anxiety to seize it, strike heavily against it and injure herself. Some falconers, however, approve of a heavy lure, as they consider that it prevents a hawk from attempting to

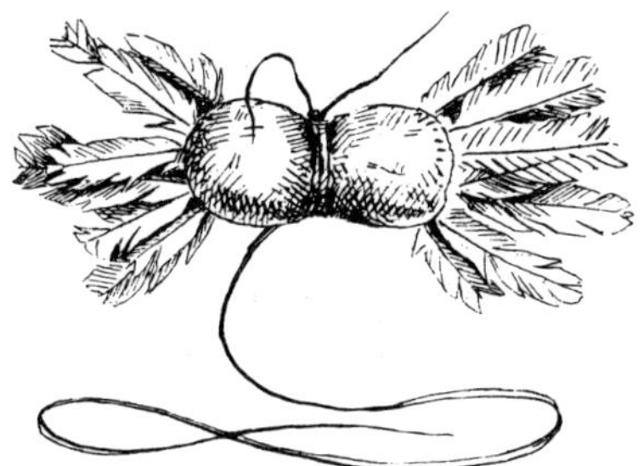

FIG. 15.—LURE FOR A MERLIN.

carry the meat away, a fault which, when once acquired, is very troublesome to cure.

This kind of lure will not do for a Merlin, being too large, and likely to repel rather than attract it. It is better to make a small bag of double wash leather, partially fill it with shot, sew it up closely, and then tie it tightly round the middle with one end of a long and strong boot-lace, until it assumes an hour-glass or dumb-bell shape (Fig. 15). Garnish each end with feathers sewn on through the quills, and tie a dog whistle at the other end of the lace. The lure is then complete, and of a size and weight to be easily carried in the pocket.

Bells.

Bells are not mere ornaments, as might be supposed; they are useful in a variety of ways.

When a hawk has "taken stand" in a tree or wood, and is concealed from view by the foliage, its whereabouts may often be ascertained by walking up wind, and listening for the bell which will sound every time the bird shifts its position. Again, when a hawk has killed at a distance, and in roots, heather, or other covert high enough to conceal it from sight, the falconer has only to mark the spot as well as he can, get there as quickly as possible, and, on drawing near, the sound of the bell as the hawk plumes the quarry will indicate its exact position.

Most hawks when first caught and tied on a perch are very restless, and will "bate off" every few minutes if not hooded (sometimes even with the hood on), experiencing a difficulty now and then in regaining the perch. The sound then produced by the violent ringing of the bell is quite different to that heard when the bird scratches the hood with one foot (as they often do), or tries to pluck off a jess. When I have had hawks on a perch in the house, I could always tell by the sound of the bell what was going on, although in another room.

Formerly a hawk carried two bells, one a semitone above the other, and, according to the "Boke of St.

Albans," bells from Milan were considered the best. At the present day in England one is considered enough.* It is put on with a little narrow strap, termed a "bewit," on one foot just above the jess, as shown in the annexed cut, though a Goshawk is sometimes belled on the tail.

When flying "at hack," that is at liberty, during the first stage of training, "eyesses" usually carry much heavier bells than those which are afterwards substituted when the birds are taken up. The

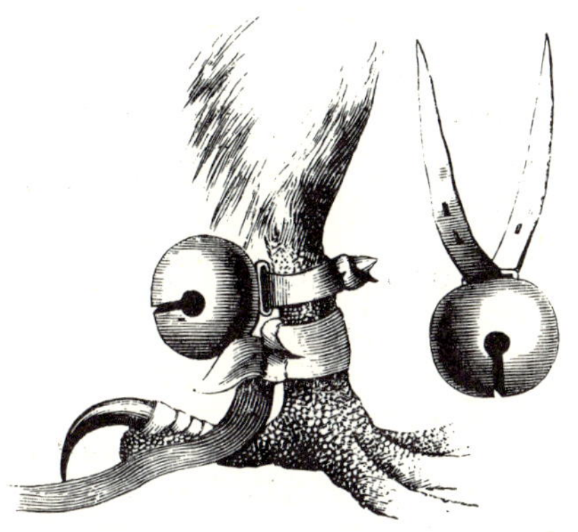

FIG. 16.—THE BELL (Dutch pattern).

former, called "hack-bells," are intended to impede the flight by their weight, and can be heard a considerable distance.

Hawks' bells are not made in England, and the small bells sold for dogs are quite useless to the falconer, for their construction does not admit of their being properly put on without chafing the birds' legs, while their sound is insignificant.

* Indian falconers use two bells.

The Dutch bells, to be obtained of Mr. K. Mollen, Valkenswaard, by Eindhoven, Holland, are very good ; but the Indian bells are most prized by modern falconers, on account of their superior tone and lightness. They are of a different shape to the Dutch bells. Instead of being spherical they are rather oval, flattened, and slightly constricted in the middle. For their size, their lightness is remarkable.

The Cadge.

The falconer's "cadge" (Fig. 17) is a useful contrivance for carrying hawks in the field. It is simply a light oblong wooden frame, with a narrow strip of carpet wrong side out, the edges turned neatly in, nailed along the upper surface to give a rough, and therefore secure, foothold to the birds while being carried.

The bearer stands in the middle, supporting a side in each hand, and generally has shoulder straps to aid him, and to allow of his letting go one hand in case a hawk bates off in a wind. Hawks should always be carried hooded when on the cadge, to prevent accident to tail and flight feathers.

Four short wooden legs attached to the underside of the frame by stiffly-working flat hinges, which admit of the legs being folded up parallel with the sides of the frame, are useful, when the cadge has to be set down, in keeping wings and tails off the ground, as shown in the annexed engraving.

When travelling by rail, another form of "cadge,"

termed a "box-cadge" is used. This is simply a deal box of a convenient length (according to the number of hawks to be carried), and of a width a little less than the door of a railway carriage, so as to admit of its passing easily through. It need not be more than twelve or fourteen inches in height. In order to afford a good grasp for the hawk's feet, a strip of wood an inch wide and half an inch thick, covered with carpet wrong side out, is screwed down on to the edge all round, projecting equally over the outside and inside of the box. Just below this so-

FIG. 17.—THE CADGE.

formed perch, in the centre of each side of the box, a circular hole, about an inch and a half in diameter, is cut with a centre bit, to enable the leash to be passed through and tied round the perch. A little sawdust is put in the box, to the depth of an inch or two, to catch the "mutes" from the birds which are tied on with their trains towards the centre, and the cadge is complete.

On a "bog-cadge" formed in this way, not more than 16in. square, four hawks, hooded, may be carried any distance by rail. If the journey be a very long one, they may be taken off by turns and carried, unhooded, on the glove.

General Management.

A newly-caught hawk should be kept on the perch for some time, hooded and unhooded, fed regularly on the hand, and carried about for a few days before it is put out on the block. If put out too soon, the tameness which it has begun to acquire is lost, and it flies wildly off the block to the end of its tether, striving vainly to make its escape, and paying no regard to lure or meat.

For the same reason, a hawk should not be bathed too soon after its arrival; but when it has come to feed well on the hand, and to take the hood well, it may be put out on the block for a few hours, and, when accustomed to this new position, it will bathe freely enough and enjoy it. The block should be set out on grass, to avoid risk of breaking wing and tail feathers, but around the base of the block a circular patch of turf may be cut out, and some sand put down to catch the "mutings," which may then be taken off the surface, when necessary, with a spade.

While on the *perch*, a hawk can only move the length of the jesses to the right or left of the swivel, turning round on the perch, and even flying off it, to return instantly. But on a *block* the hawk has nearly the length of the leash to fly, and, supposing this to represent a radius of 2ft. from the ring of the block, the leash itself when untied being about a yard long, the bird can describe a good circle.

It is most important to see that the leash is properly tied to the block. For want of this precaution, many a bird has made its escape, taking the leash with it, by means of which it has perhaps got entangled in some tree, and so come to an untimely and miserable death. Falconers make a particular knot for this purpose (already described p. 26). This is done with the right hand only, while the left holds the bird, which should not be unhooded until it has been set down on the block, after the knot has been tied. As it is not easy to describe a knot, even with the aid of an illustration, the novice would do well to acquire the knack of making knots (there are several used by falconers) by watching the movements of a practised hand, and then try to imitate them.

On setting a hawk down on a block, one or two points should be carefully attended to. In the first place, the spot selected should be as quiet as possible, and out of the way of stray dogs and cats; although, if the falconer have a spaniel or two (as is advisable for game hawking), they may be easily accustomed to the hawks, and the hawks to them, by letting them out when the bird is on the glove, and therefore out of their reach, and less likely to be alarmed at their appearance. By holding one of the birds with the hood on close to the dog, with words of caution, the latter will soon learn what is expected of him. But it is one thing to have your own dogs on terms with your hawks, and another thing to expect good behaviour from other people's dogs.

As they cannot be depended upon, proper precautions must be taken; and the same may be said with regard to cats. In the next place, care should be taken not to set down the block in a hot sun, but rather where some shelter from the sun's rays may be obtained. Peregrines especially seem to prefer shade. I have often observed them leaving the block, which had become too hot to be agreeable, and cowering on the shadow of the block projected on the grass, when that was the only shade they could reach. They will be none the worse for sitting out in the rain, provided there be no very cold wind at the time. In their natural state, of course, hawks are exposed to all weathers, and have often to sit out a gale or a snowstorm. But then, be it remembered, they are able to take active exercise immediately afterwards, dry their feathers, and restore impeded circulation. It is the want of these advantages that renders it desirable to take more care of hawks in captivity than would otherwise be necessary.

On no account should a bird that has got a soaking in the rain be put near the fire to dry. It should be brought in and put upon the perch out of all draught, where it will sit for some time, "mantling" and "rousing" (*i.e.*, stretching its wings and shaking its feathers) until dry again.

To Keep a Hawk in Health.

There are three requisites for keeping a hawk in health—proper food given at the right time and in the proper quantity, an occasional bath, and frequent exercise. As regards food, Peregrines thrive best on lean beef, with an occasional pigeon, or a bit of young rabbit, or the head and neck of a fowl smashed up with a mallet. Merlins require food that is more easily digested, and should be fed on sheep's heart, with a small bird or mouse now and then for casting.* Of course, after a bird has been trained, it may be fed on the quarry it kills, and Merlins are never in better health than when they are living chiefly on the larks they have taken.

I have said that Merlins may be fed twice a day, morning and evening; Peregrines, unless they be eyesses, once only, in the evening. It is important to bear in mind that a "casting" should never be given in the morning; that is to say, if you give a Merlin a light meal in the morning, care should be taken to remove all feathers, fur, and bones, otherwise the meal would not be digested, and the "casting," or "pellet," thrown up in time for the bird to be hungry enough to be flown in the afternoon.

When flying Merlins in August and September, my plan was to go out before breakfast with a gun and shoot a few larks on the stubble. I used then to skin them, and give only the meat off each side of the breast-bone, taking care that there were no grains of shot in it, and making each hawk come off the perch to the lure for it. The perch was rigged up in an empty stable, wherein they were left untied all night. If it can be managed, Merlins are

* The particular treatment of Merlins is described farther on.

all the better for not being tied. After feeding in the morning, I used to put them down on their blocks on the grass, and give them each a bath in turn, taking the bath away as soon as the bird was out of it. I then found that by two or three o'clock in the afternoon they were quite dry, keen, and ready to fly. At this time, of course, they were trained, and would come well to the swung lure—the best mode of exercising hawks.

Training.

But the novice will naturally say, How do you train them, and how soon may they be trusted on the wing? Well, the process is not a difficult one, and only requires the exercise of gentleness and patience. Bearing in mind what has been said about feeding a newly-caught hawk on the glove or on the lure, it will be found that the bird when hungry, will readily jump from the perch, or block, to the hand, or on the lure, if the latter be thrown on the ground. All that is then necessary is to remove the leash and tie a long light line to the swivel (which remains attached to the jesses during the training, but never when the trained hawk is flown), and holding this line (a plaited fishing line is best) in the left hand when the hawk is called off to the lure, the length of flight may be increased daily, until finally the line may be dispensed with altogether. It is important to bear in mind that the hawk should never be flown except when it is hungry, and when

Setting Down a Hawk on the Block.

it is therefore most likely to be obedient to the lure. Before discarding the line, or "creance," as it is technically termed, a live bird, of the kind to be afterwards flown at, should be given in a shorter creance, and the hawk allowed not only to kill it, but to make a good meal off it. When it has been struck down, the falconer should never approach hastily and take it away, or lift the hawk up with it, but on the contrary, should stand at a little distance, and allow the hawk to break well into the "quarry." It may then be approached gently, and the falconer, kneeling down with a bit of meat on his glove, or on the lure, should present this to the hawk *over* the bird it has killed, and is still holding. The hawk will then take a mouthful or two, and will gradually grasp and step up on the lure or glove, allow itself to be lifted up, and continue feeding as long as desirable, until the hood is slipped on.

If an untrained hawk be approached suddenly on killing a bird, it will either try to carry it away, or will let go and fly away without it. This fault, termed "carrying," is a troublesome one to cure if once contracted, but, with proper care at starting, and attention to the hints above given, this danger may be obviated.

The First Flight.

When flying a hawk loose for the first time, it is most important to guard against a disappointment, and care should be taken to secure such a flight that the hawk will be almost certain to kill. The method I pursue with a Merlin is to carry it hooded over likely ground for a Lark, until I put one up. As soon as it has pitched again and I have marked it down, I take off the hood and walk straight up wind to the spot. The Lark again rises, the hawk is off the hand in a second, and, if previously well exercised to the lure, is almost sure to kill. I then allow her to plume the quarry and have a few mouthfuls before I take her up, letting her finish the meal on my glove. In this way she gains confidence. It is just as well not to essay more than one flight the first day, especially if the first flight results in a kill. A Lark will often "ring up" to a good height, and the first flight may sometimes be enough for a beginning. Later on, as the hawk improves, one may have two or three flights of an afternoon with the same hawk, remembering not to feed her much between each flight.

To kill a Rook or a Partridge with a Peregrine is a very different matter, and not nearly so easy of accomplishment. The *modus operandi*, too, varies in several respects, and will be described in detail later on. I am here writing hints for beginners, and, the Merlin being more easily trained than any other hawk, it is advisable to commence with this bird. More ambitious flights should be postponed until the first lesson has been well learnt.

To Snare a Shy Hawk.

Should a hawk, on being flown loose for the first time, prove shy and difficult to take up, it should be snared to prevent risk of losing it ; and the simplest plan is to peg down a long fishing line with an open knot in it, in the centre of which is placed a lark (for a Merlin) or a pigeon (for a Peregrine). A couple of feathers stuck in the ground, sloping towards the centre of the noose, will cause the line when pulled to slip up over the bait and secure the hawk round the legs. Another plan, called "winding up," is to peg down a long line, and, throwing out the lure, allow the hawk to take it; then, holding the long line, describe a wide circle round the peg twice, and draw tight, when the hawk will be snared round the legs. Some further hints on snaring will be found hereafter in the chapter "Devices for Taking Hawks."

Coping.

A freshly caught hawk, especially if a passage hawk, has beak and claws as hard and sharp as needles, easily driven through any ordinary glove. The tips of these (about the eighth of an inch) may be easily removed with a pair of cutting pliers, as the hawk sits hooded on the perch. But great care must be taken in "coping" the beak in this way, lest a sudden wrench of the bird's head should splinter the beak on one side. In case of such an accident, the broken edge must be carefully taken down with a small file.

Imping.

A broken flight feather, or tail feather, may be repaired by obtaining a corresponding feather from the wing or tail of a dead or stuffed hawk of the same species, cutting it to the right length, cutting the ends of the old and new feathers which are to meet, with a similar slope, so that they come together neatly with the webs of both of equal width, and then thrusting a short three-edged needle pointed at both ends (called an imping-needle) half-way into each quill, and pushing the latter gently and firmly together. If the needle be previously dipped in brine, it will, by subsequently rusting, keep a firmer hold in the quill. This operation, called "imping," (from A.S. *impan*, to graft), requires some practice to perform it neatly, and the bird should be hooded and held down on a soft cushion by an assistant. Imping-needles may be obtained from Mr. Ashton (Whitesmith), Feltwell, Brandon, Suffolk.

Moulting.

Hawks are very uncertain in the time and duration of their moult, which is doubtless retarded by confinement. As a rule, they commence to cast their feathers in April, and are clean moulted early in October. In other words, they moult all through the summer, shedding their feathers gradually, and in pairs. This is necessitated by the very nature of their habits, for, were they in a wild state to lose all their quill feathers at once, like wild mallards (which, being of aquatic habits, can live without them for a time) they would be at once incapacitated from getting a living.

The nestling plumage is retained until the following spring, that is to say, a hawk does not begin to moult until it is nearly a year old. Usually the moult is commenced early in April and completed in October. The feathers are shed, or "cast," in pairs, the first to drop out being the seventh flight feather in each wing, and the last to be shed is the first primary in each wing. Similarly the *centre* feathers of the tail (the "deck feathers," as they are termed) are cast before the *outside* ones, the reason being that the outside feathers, both in wings and tail, are strong and flexible, and so give support to the tender growing feathers which come down between them. As already hinted, the reason for the lengthened period over which the moult is extended, and for the new feathers coming down in pairs is that the hawk may never be disabled from getting its living, as would be the case if (like certain water-fowl) all the quills were moulted about the same time.

Some falconers copy nature, and exercise their hawks all through the moult; others deem it better to turn them loose in a warm loft with a perch at either end, and a bath in the middle, and keep them in high condition until clean moulted. The latter plan, of course, implies the loss of their services during a certain time of year peculiarly favourable to game hawking. We read in the "Boke of St. Alban's," 1486, that—

> "Who so puttyth his hawke in mewe in the begynnynge of Lente, if she be kepte as she ought to be, she shall be mewyd in the begynnynge of August."

This, however, is not the experience of modern falconers. The Spanish falconers of old were wont to say that the Peregrines bred in the South of Europe commence to moult sooner and get through the moult quicker than any others, and both Pero Lopez de Ayala and Juan de Sant-Fahagun state that they have seen Peregrines that were clean moulted and killing herons by the end of July and beginning of August.

Medicines.

Old writers on falconry give a multiplicity of recipes for curing all sorts of diseases, real or imaginary, some of them very extraordinary in regard to the ingredients. No English falconers of the present day believe in them, and there can be no doubt that the less medicine given the better. In a state of nature hawks cannot procure drugs, and would not touch them if they could. They keep themselves in health by exercise, bathing, and freshly-killed warm food. There was much sense in the characteristic reply made by the old Scotch falconer, Peter Ballantine, who, when asked "the best medicine for a sick hawk," said, "d—— yer medicines, gie 'em a warm doo"—a freshly-killed pigeon being undoubtedly, in his opinion, the best kind of physic. Nevertheless, there are times when a little stimulant, or a slight purge, will do good. For a cold and sneezing, or cough (technically called "croaks") two or three peppercorns may be given one after another concealed in morsels of meat, with good effect, care being taken to keep the bird moderately warm, and fed on light and nourishing food.

When the stomach is disordered, as indicated by the appearance of the "mutes" and "castings," a little powdered rhubarb, enveloped in a bit of meat, will do good. But, as a rule, physicking should be avoided, and to restore health only such means should be resorted to as are likely to be available in a state of nature.

Indian Recipe to Purge a Hawk of Fat.

I am indebted to an enthusiastic falconer, General Griffiths, formerly Colonel commanding the 3rd Sikhs in India, for the following native recipe for purging a hawk of fat:—"Salamoniac, as we get it, is in pieces like the inside edible part of a cocoa-nut. Take a piece the size of half-a-crown, put it on the fire in butter sufficient to cover it, and fry it well. When it begins to turn black, remove it from the fire, and take it out of the butter with a pair of pincers; hot, and pour over it the juice of a fresh lime or lemon. When cool put it in a stoppered bottle, and it will keep for years."

"For use, take a piece as big as the top of your little finger ◯, wrap it in cotton wool lightly, tie round gently with thread, and it is ready. The day before giving the dose the falcon should have only well washed meat, and very little of it. Get an assistant to cast and hold her. Then open her mouth and drop in half a teaspoonful of water luke-warm. Then give the ball, and with your little finger push it well past the crop and into the gullet.

Put on the hood and set her up. Do not draw the hood tight. Stroke her and shake her to prevent her disgorging under abour 8 or 10 minutes; then let her cast. Sometimes the fat comes up with the medicine, sometimes after." General Griffiths adds :—"It has happened to me that the fat has not come up. In this case I have given a ball again in half an hour, but this very seldom occurs. After the dose watch the mutes for about two hours, when they will become white. Give three or four pecks of blood, cutting a pigeon's throat for the purpose, and in the evening give a small feed of well washed meat, about as much as a sparrow. The next day also a light feed of washed meat, and fly the day after. The fat removed is a regular film, $\frac{1}{8}$in. thick, sac-shaped, and quite green."

In India this dose is given to a Saker every three weeks, certainly every month, or it would fly away. In England experience has proved that the Peregrine may be trained to kill rooks, partridges, and grouse to perfection, without recourse to any such physic.

Maxims for Falconers.

1. Gentleness before all. Hawks when first caught are very timid, and should never be unnecessarily alarmed or frightened by approaching them too suddenly, or taking them hurriedly off the perch. By degrees they should be accustomed to be stroked—at first with a broad feather or pinion, and after-

wards with the hand. In this way they will learn to overcome their fear at the sight of an approaching hood.

2. Hoods should never be left out at night, for if they get wet the braces swell, and they won't draw. They should be kept in a moderately dry place, the braces slightly greased from time to time to make them draw easily, and when not in use the hood should be closed to preserve its shape.

3. Always carry a spare hood or two in the field, in case of loss or accident. As regards the colour of the eyepiece, *red* is preferable to *green*, as being more easily seen at a distance if dropped on the grass.

4. Never feed a hawk (except a Merlin) on the morning of the day on which she is to be flown; and if a "casting" has been given the day before, see that the pellet has been thrown up the following morning—for not until this has been got rid off will the hawk be fit to fly. If a live or recently killed bird, or other animal cannot be readily procured when wanted for "casting," a handful of small feathers well mixed up with chopped lean beef, may be given, and will be readily taken; but in this case the meat, being easily pulled to pieces, should be held firmly in the glove to prevent the hawk from feeding too fast.

5. When bathing a hawk remove the leash by which it is always carried, and tied to perch

or block, and substitute an old but sound leash, or bit of plaited blind-cord. A good leash may soon be spoiled by constant wetting and drying.

6. Never attempt to fly a hawk in the rain, or in a high wind, unless you want to lose it. Some hawks will not pursue in the rain, nor come down to a dead lure if it be thrown on the wet grass. If allowed to get away too far down wind, and the wind be at all high, they will not persevere in trying to work back against it to the lure.*

7. As a hawk on attaining her "pitch" almost invariably works down wind, take care that in that direction there is no such obstacle as a large wood, a sheet of water, or a river which you cannot cross without going perhaps a mile out of the way for a bridge.

---

* The writer was once training a young falcon and tiercel on Staines Moor. The wind was rather high. The falcon, being a larger and stronger bird, came back to the lure pretty well; but the tiercel, being a small light bird, seemed to experience great difficulty in flying up wind, every now and then veering off, and being carried away like a feather for a considerable distance. A flock of house pigeons appearing on the wing most inopportunely down wind, the temptation was irresistable. Away went the tiercel in pursuit, chased them out of sight, and was never seen again. A long search down wind till dark, and renewed at daybreak, was ineffectual. A reward of £1 was offered through the police for information which might lead to its recovery, and a week afterwards the bell was received by post, with a note from the superintendent of police, intimating that the hawk had been shot by a gardener at Eltham as it sat in a tree close to his employer's house. This suggested the maxim, "If the wind be high, do not fly."

8. Always approach the quarry up wind, and fly a hawk into the wind to help her to mount.
9. If a hawk be lost, search should be made a long way down wind in the direction she was last seen to take. If rooks or jackdaws take the air and continue circling at a height with loud "caws," they will generally indicate the whereabouts of the fugitive. If she has killed a rook or other bird, as often happens, she should be allowed to break well into it before being taken up. If, on the contrary, she has taken stand in some tree, she may be lured off, down wind, with a live pigeon in a string.
10. When putting up temporarily at an inn or at a friend's house, where there is no accommodation for hawks, care should be taken not to place a bird where she can injure herself, or break her flight feathers by striking them against chair-backs, or sharp corners. It is safer to peg her down by her leash on the lawn, and give her a large inverted flower pot for a block. In this case see that there are no stray cats or dogs about.
11. Many a hawk has got away and been lost from not being properly tied at the block. Care should always be taken in tying the leash, and the knack of making "the falconer's knot" should be acquired as soon as possible.
12. *Ne quid nimis.* Do not keep too many hawks at a time. Two or three good birds will show more sport than half-a-dozen imperfectly trained ones.

The Secret of Success.

What the falconer has to aim at in the field is to make his hawk understand that he does not approach her to take away the food from her, but to help her to secure and enjoy it. As soon as that feeling is established between bird and man, all will go well. The hawk will improve daily, and the falconer's pleasure will be proportionally increased.

A French writer on Falconry has well said:

"Toute la science de la Fauconnerie ne consiste qu'à tenir les oiseaux pleins et en bon état, c'est-à-dire à bien voler et à donner du plaisir à leur maitre."*

Before concluding this portion of the subject I cannot do better than reiterate the excellent advice given by one of the most successful falconers of the present day, Mr. W. H. St. Quintin, of Scampston Hall, Yorkshire, when announcing the list of quarry killed by his hawks in the season of 1893-94 (*The Field*, June 2, 1894):

"Beginners," he says, "should firstly make up their minds what species of quarry their surrounding circumstances give them the best prospect of pursuing with success, stick to that, and that alone, for at least their first season Secondly, they should not attempt to keep too many hawks—one or, at the most, two, are quite enough for a beginner to try his 'prentice hand' upon.

"My own belief is that, for his first season at least, a beginner, unless exceptionally favourably situated, will do well to commence

---

* Ch. de Morais, "Le Veritable Fauconnier," 1683.

with the Goshawk or with Merlins, before undertaking the more difficult flights with the Peregrine. But, if he must have a Peregrine, and I can myself entirely sympathise with his preference for this more noble bird, let it be an eyess, and, if possible, by the assistance of some friend of more experience, one already properly hacked, and made to hood and lure. Such was the procedure which was recommended to me some fifteen years ago by some friends who had long made their reputations as successful falconers, and I have often congratulated myself on my good fortune in having met with such sensible and practical advice. Nowadays I fear too many would-be falconers are in too great a hurry to run before they can walk, and, as it seems to me, they are prone to waste their time and money, and, as a result, too often get utterly discouraged, by, at the outset, attempting too much, and with unsuitable material.

"The beginner must not feel discouraged if he only succeeds in bringing very little 'to bag' during his first season. That period will be profitably spent if, at the end of it, he finds that he has become fairly skilful in handling his (eyess) hawk, in hooding, feeding, and imping, and if he has acquired some knowledge of the mysteries of condition, and of the management of his hawk in mews, at the block, and in the field; also—quite as important—how best to circumvent his selected quarry. This experience gained, he may presently proceed to other more difficult flights, and to try his hand with hawks that require more experience if full justice is to be done them."

The Triumph of Art.

Few persons, except those who have experienced it, can realise the feelings of a falconer when flying a hawk which he has tamed and trained himself. To see a brace of well-trained pointers or setters quarter their ground, stand, back, and drop to shot, returning from a distance obedient to their owner's whistle, is, undoubtedly, a grand sight, and one to gladden the heart of any man who has the faintest love of sport in his nature; but to see a falcon leave her owner's hand, take the air, and, mounting with the greatest ease, fly straight away at the rate of a mile a minute, and then at a whistle, or a whoop, and a toss of the lure, turn in her flight and come out of the clouds to his hand, is to see a triumph of man's art in subduing the lower animals, and making them obedient to his will. The wonder is that so fascinating a sport as that of hawking has ever ceased to be popular.

PRACTICAL FALCONRY.

CHAPTERS HISTORICAL AND DESCRIPTIVE.

"Thus have I politicly begun my reign,
And 'tis my hope to end successfully.
My falcon now is sharp and passing empty;
And till she stoop she must not be full-gorged,
For then she never looks upon her lure."

Taming of the Shrew. Act iv., sc. 1.

ROOK HAWKING.

NO one from casual observation of the bird's habits would think of crediting the Rook with great powers of flight. To watch him from the roadside as he drops heavily into an adjacent meadow, whence, after marching about for some time in quest of food, solemnly nodding his head at every step, he betakes himself with slowly flapping wing to the nearest tree, it would never be supposed that he could show sport to a falconer, or hold his own for a minute when pursued by a hawk.

But see him out on the open downs a mile or two from home, where he has to take long flights to and from the rookery in order to get his living; he is then in fine flying order and good condition, and can travel down wind at a pace that will astonish a mounted horseman who goes out for the first time to see a "flight."

As a matter of fact, it has been calculated by Sir George Cayley* that a Rook usually flies at the rate of about 35ft. per second, the weight and wing area

---

* "On Aerial Navigation," in Nicholson's Journ. Nat. Phil. xxiv., p. 164, quoted by Prof. Roy in Newton's "Dictionary of Birds," art. "Flight."

being, roughly speaking, in the ratio of one pound to the square foot. This calculation credits the Rook with a speed of about 24 miles per hour as compared with 36 miles per hour, the estimated speed of a homing pigeon. (See the *Field*, 22 Jan., 1887, p. 114.)

In a state of nature it is very doubtful whether the Rook often falls a prey to the Falcon, notwithstanding the comparative ease with which it might be captured. Were it otherwise, we should see much more frequently than is the case the half-picked remains of rooks lying about in the open, showing where the hawk had been at work. Instead of this, what do we find? The remains of wood pigeons, stockdoves, partridges, peewits, anything rather than rooks, from which we are forced to conclude that, unless a Falcon is very sharp set, she has no natural enmity to the Rook, and no particular liking for this quarry when anything better is to be obtained. And no wonder, for it must be admitted by all who have tasted rook-pie in the spring that a pigeon-pie, or a roasted partridge, would be infinitely preferable. More than this, there is a seeming distaste on the part of the Peregrine Falcon for the flesh of the Rook, as is evident from the reluctance which is shown by the latter (when trained) to fly this quarry. Some hawks, indeed, can never be got to take rooks, or are only induced to do so by the exercise of skill and stratagem on the part of the falconer, as will presently be shown. Before a hawk, therefore, can be successfully flown at a rook—that is to say, flown so as to pursue it with ardour, and either kill it or put it into covert and be taken down with a lure—a great deal has to be done in the way of training, over and above what is necessary to make a hawk fly well to the lure as already described. In the first place she must be properly entered to rooks, and for that purpose a live rook or two must be procured. There are several ways of getting them. One plan is to set a snaring line over a nest when it is re-visited in February or March for repairs, the line being pulled from below when the bird has entered it. Another plan, and a very old one, is to smear the inside of some brown paper cones with bird lime, and to plant them at intervals on ground frequented by rooks, dropping a few grains of corn into each as a bait. The birds, in attempting to reach the grain get hoodwinked with the cones, which stick fast to the feathers of the head, and, after a short erratic flight, they come to the ground, and may be picked up. A third plan is to tie a small piece of meat at one end of a short string, and a stone or weight at the other, smearing the string with bird lime. The rook on flying away with the meat causes the stone to swing like a pendulum, and the sticky line catching the feathers sooner or later brings the bird down. But perhaps the simplest plan of all is to set a few gins behind a plough when the rooks are eagerly following the team to pick up worms and larvæ from the newly turned soil. In this way a rook may be easily captured. An Irish plover catcher, E. Dwyer, of Stradavoher, Thurles, stated that he could catch rooks when flying low against the wind with a net 18 feet long by 7 feet deep.

But, a Rook not being the natural prey of a Falcon, the latter will often require some little coaxing before she will seize one. Before entering her, therefore, at this quarry it is well to feed her for some time previously on very dark-coloured pigeons, or to give her the leg of a black plumaged fowl to "tire" on, and when she has eventually killed her first rook (with a line on) a freshly killed pigeon should be adroitly thrust up from under the rook's outstretched wings, and cut open in such a way as as to enable the hawk to get a mouthful of pigeon instead of rook. In this way a hawk that is at first rook-shy may be gradually brought to overcome her reluctance to take this sable quarry, and eventually to fly it eagerly.

Assuming that the entering process has been successfully carried out with the aid of a lure, the hawk may then be flown loose, and the first chance given her should be an easy one. A successful flight at a Rook requires more preparation than, perhaps, many a young falconer would imagine. In the first place, the hawk, which has been fed about 5 p.m. the previous day, and has been on the perch all night, must be looked to in the morning about 7 or 8 a.m., to see if she has got rid of her "casting." That having been found on the clean sand, or sawdust, beneath the perch (the former for choice, as it does not get so scattered about, and does not hold the moisture and smell as sawdust does) the hawk is untied, taken off on the glove with just a pull of meat by way of enticement, hooded, and carried out to the block on the lawn, where she is set down, and properly tied with the leash to the ring of the block. The bath is then set down close by, and the hood removed, the falconer retiring to a little distance. After bathing, the hawk will return to the block and sit mantling, rousing, and preening her feathers until she is dry again. About eleven

FIG. 18.—A GOOD ROOK HAWK.

o'clock, when she has become keen and ready for a flight, she may be hooded up, and, after sitting quiet for a time, may be carried to the field.

There is this essential difference between "game hawking" and "rook hawking." In the former case the hawk is put on the wing and allowed to mount to a good height before the birds are flushed down wind of her (whether they have been marked down, or are to be found with dogs): in the latter case the rooks are found well out in the open, and are to be approached up wind, with the hawk upon the glove and hooded: the hood is not removed until the rooks rise, when the hawk is immediately slipped, and is then said to be flown "out of the hood," instead of being "put up." It is important to see that the rooks are in a good position for a flight, that they are well up wind of you, and that there is no covert for some considerable distance down wind of them; the reason for this being that a Rook, on being chased by a Falcon, after "ringing up" and trying in vain to keep above the hawk (though sometimes succeeding in doing so), will turn tail and go down wind as fast as he can fly to the nearest covert, which may be copse, farm buildings, wheat stack, or even a sheepfold—anywhere to avoid the merciless stoop of the Falcon.

On preparing to "hood off" at a Rook, the young falconer must remember several things: First, to approach up wind; secondly, if there be a fresh breeze blowing, and the hawk, being keen, is inclined to "bate," to screen her as much as possible from the rooks, and keep her bell quiet; thirdly, to be ready to slip her at a moment's notice. With this object the leash may be put in the pocket, the swivel detached from the jesses, which must be very securely held by thumb and forefinger, the ends held also between middle and third finger, and the braces of the hood half drawn to admit of its being pulled off by the plume as soon as the rooks rise. As to the distance at which a hawk may be slipped, that will depend upon circumstances. A young and inexperienced hawk may have a short slip to begin with, say sixty or seventy yards. After a few flights, the rooks themselves generally take care that the slip shall be a long one. It is astonishing at what a distance a hawk will go up to her rooks when she has had a few good flights, and found that she can catch and kill them: she then thinks nothing of a quarter of a mile slip. In 1890, 258 Rooks were taken with the hawks belonging to the Old Hawking Club: in an average year, 150-160.

When rooks take the air at the sight of an approaching hawk, an indescribable scene of confusion ensues. Rising with loud and angry caws, the black crowd at first disperses in all directions, mounting higher and higher, until at length, finding only one of their number pursued, they draw together again, and, still at a great height, continue to sail round in circles, giving vent at intervals to their displeasure. Meantime the hawk, having been cast off against the wind, is buoyantly lifted, and, going straight into the wind, is soon at a fair height. Coming round again down wind at a tremendous pace, and once more turning, she is again carried to a greater elevation, until at length, in two or three rings, she has gained her "pitch," and then, as a sailor would say, "look out for squalls." Fixing her attention on one particular rook—not always the easiest one to take—away she goes in hot pursuit, the Rook doing his very best to keep above in order to avoid the fatal stoop that may send him tumbling to earth. If baulked in this, he will try what shifting will do. Down comes the Falcon with half-closed wings; the Rook wrenches to one side, or drops a little, the hawk dashes by, missing him only by a few inches; but instantly "throwing up" is again at the elevation from which she descended, and is ready to repeat the manœuvre. Another grand "stoop," and this time a few feathers are knocked out, showing what a near thing it was for the Rook. The latter, finding it impossible to keep above the hawk, turns down wind and makes for the nearest covert, whatever it may be—a barn, a rick yard, or a clump of trees in the distance. Away he goes as fast as he can fly, the hawk close behind and slightly above him, the excited falconers galloping below at their best pace to keep both hawk and quarry in view. The covert is nearly reached; it looks as if the Rook would save himself after all; but, within fifty yards of the friendly shelter, the hawk makes a splendid effort—a headlong downward rush—and the rook, seized by one wing, comes tumbling down in the grasp of his pursuer. The field come galloping up, and, dismounting at a short distance, a falconer approaches to take up the hawk. In the case of an experienced bird, he can do this at once without risk of her "carrying" or going away; but if the hawk has been but recently "entered" to rooks, he must be cautious; approach slowly, giving her time to kill and break into the quarry, and finally with a piece of meat in his glove, or a dead pigeon, he may go down on one knee, and, pushing forward the meat towards her, allow her to pull at it and seize it with one foot, which she will readily do, when, getting hold of the ends of the jesses, she may be lifted gently on to the glove and hooded. Taken back to the cadge, she is allowed a rest, and another hawk is got ready for the next flight.

Should the Rook, however, make good his escape, either by ringing up or putting into some shelter from which he cannot be dislodged, the hawk must be taken down to the lure, rewarded with a mouthful or two, hooded up, and restored to the cadge.

The cadge should be set down in a sheltered spot out of the wind, or, better still, carried in a light covered cart. To carry the bird on a cadge in a cold wind across an open down, bating and struggling to hold on, is by no means conducive to subsequent good flying.

Sometimes a hawk, on being disappointed of a "kill," will make away down wind at a great pace in search of some other quarry. Perhaps she will spy a lot of rooks down wind of her, and go away and kill one of them before the falconer can get up. Then she has to be looked for, her line of flight noted, and the position of the rook's companions observed; for, when one of their number has been cut down they will soar round and round above the spot, and indicate by their actions that the hawk is below them. Then, if she cannot be seen at once, her bell must be listened for, when, guided by the sound, the falconer will soon walk on to her and take her up.

Rook hawking is the only branch of the sport in

which riding is nowadays necessary, unless, when in search of rooks, a stone curlew or Norfolk plover may rise from a fallow or stony portion of the down and go right away. For game hawking, riding is generally unnecessary for partridges and impracticable for grouse, from the nature of the ground; although in wide open partridge ground, where the fields of roots are large—sometimes 80 to 100 acres—a cob is useful to carry the falconer round the outside into the wind, so as to cast off his hawk properly; as well as to enable him to take up the hawk if she has killed or put in any great distance from him.

The best kind of horse for hawking is a short-legged, steady little horse that can jump a bit—short-legged to enable the rider to get on and off quickly, and steady enough to stand quiet while the falconer takes up the hawk. To assist this the saddle should have a holster carrying a long weight like a clock weight. This, fastened by a cord from the pommel through the ring of the bit, may then be thrown on the ground to tether the horse when the falconer dismounts.

October is the season for getting Rook-hawks. They are then caught by the Dutch hawk-catchers at Valkenswaard, in North Brabant, and the usual consignment to English falconers generally takes place towards the end of November. By the time they reach England, as they usually do, in the care of the falconer of the Old Hawking Club, who annually journeys to Holland to bring over eight for the Club, they have been broken to the hood, well handled, fed every day on the fist, and are generally in a condition to be taken in hand by a purchaser, and either made or marred. Directions for dealing with a new purchase of this sort have already been given. The reader who may be anxious to procure one or more should write in September or October to Mr. Mollen, Valkenswaard, by Eindhoven, Holland, and state his requirements. The cost of a passage falcon is £4, and of a tiercel £3, hood, jesses, and leash being included, and the mode of transport to England in November may be easily arranged with the falconer of the Old Hawking Club by permission of the Hon. Secretary.

Doubtless a less expensive plan is to procure eyess falcons in this country at a cost of, say, £1 apiece, or less in out of the way parts of the country, where hawks do not command a ready sale. In Scotland and Wales, for example, I have known three eyesses from one nest willingly parted with for a sovereign.

In fair weather eyesses will sometimes kill Rooks well enough, but, generally speaking, they have not the dash, and determination in sticking to a Rook, that a passage hawk displays—a qualification so necessary when flying on the wide, open downs during the cold winds of March. They are better suited for game, and for "partridge hawking" the best birds I ever saw were eyess tiercels.

Some years ago, when spending much time every autumn in West Sussex, at the foot of the downs, and in a good partridge country, I kept both falcons and tiercels for partridge hawking, and two of the latter, "Redcap" and "Robin Hood," were as good as one could wish, turning and stooping much quicker than the falcons. The latter, however, from their superior size and strength, were preferable for rook hawking.*

---

* One of these falcons, "Dutch Lady," flown at a Rook from the down near Up Park, went to Midhurst (about eight miles), where she was shot, while holding a Rook on the ground in Cowdray Park, by a keeper of Lord Egmont, before she could be taken up. In reply to my remonstrance, his lordship sent me a courteous letter regretting the keeper's want of discrimination, and enclosing the bell (broken by the shot), while the unfortunate hawk was stuffed for the keeper by the village saddler! Lest it should be inferred from this incident that a flight at a Rook may sometimes last for eight miles, it should be observed that this can very rarely happen. The Rook is either stricken down within a mile or two of where the hawk has been slipped, or saves itself by "putting in" to covert. On the occasion above referred to, the hawk was flown on the South Downs at a considerable elevation above the valley; the Rook "flown at" saved itself by "putting in" at Elstead, and the hawk, sighting other rooks down wind, went away in pursuit, and killed one in the park at Cowdray, with the disastrous result above stated.

PARTRIDGE HAWKING.

To witness the stoop of a well-trained falcon at a fast-flying partridge or grouse, as it goes down wind at the highest speed of which it is capable, is a sight to be for ever remembered. Sportsmen who know what it is to shoot driven birds, and who are wont to estimate the speed of a partridge at forty, fifty, or even sixty miles an hour, incline to the belief that a driven partridge must be the fastest bird that flies, and few are prepared to learn that neither a partridge nor a grouse can live long before a Peregrine Falcon. There is a popular notion, and a pretty theory that hawks are "Nature's police;" that they carry off the weakly birds of a covey, and so, by allowing the strongest and best to escape, they help to maintain a good healthy stock of game. This is an absolute fallacy. Having seen scores of grouse and partridges taken by trained falcons, I am in a position to assert positively that the power of wing in a Peregrine is so great, that it can overtake and strike down the strongest and best bird in a covey with as much ease as if it were the youngest and weakliest of the brood. It might naturally be supposed that on the rising of a covey, the hawk would stoop at the bird nearest to it. This is not invariably the case. I have many times seen a falcon ignore a grouse immediately under her, and single out for capture either the leader of the pack, or an outside bird far ahead of some of its fellows.* It is the same in partridge-hawking. The hawk probably stoops at the bird of which it first catches sight when the covey rises. Just as in partridge shooting, the sportsman singles out the bird he first sees on the wing, unless it happens to be too near him, when he aims at one further away by which time the bird first seen will be at a proper distance for his second barrel.

It will be inferred from what has been already stated that the modes of flying a short-winged hawk and a long-winged falcon are entirely different. In the former case the quarry is found before the hawk leaves the fist; in the latter, the falcon is put on the wing and allowed to "mount" to a good "pitch" before the dogs are allowed to range. As soon as they are steady on point, and the falcon well placed overhead, the birds are flushed, and the falcon, immediately catching sight of them, with a headlong rush, stoops at the one she has singled out. So truly is she a judge of pace and distance, that, unless the partridge drops suddenly into covert, she rarely fails to strike it fatally. No prettier picture could present itself to the eye of an artist than the grouping of dogs, hawk, and falconer at the moment which precedes the fatal stoop. The dogs

* In this I am borne out by every falconer of my acquaintance who has seen a trained Peregrine kill grouse.

—setters or spaniels as the case may be—motionless on point, half-concealed perhaps in a field of turnips, or patch of clover, or standing out in bold relief upon the edge of a stubble; the hawk, well understanding the proceedings, "waiting on" at a considerable height above them; the falconers, advancing slowly in line, or pausing in their enthusiasm

FIG. 19.—A GOOD SPANIEL FOR PARTRIDGES.

to admire the scene before them. A step forward, a rush of wings, a shout of "Hoo, ha, ha," a grey meteor falls across the sky, and amid a small cloud of feathers a partridge drops with a dull thud amongst the turnip leaves, or, like a stone in water, disappears in the waving clover.

A *finale* such as this, however, is not to be effected as a matter of course by any tyro who can procure a hawk. Its accomplishment implies a great deal of previous trouble in the taming, training, feeding, bathing, and general management of the noble falcon before it can be trusted to fly at liberty, and exhibit the exercise of its natural instinct for man's pleasure and benefit.

It would be impossible within the limits of the present chapter to give a detailed account of the mode of training game-hawks ; but, with a view to encourage attempts on the part of those who have leisure and inclination for such sport, it will not be out of place to offer a few remarks upon the more important points to be attended to.

It may be stated, then, as a general principle, which underlies the whole art of falconry, that a hawk is flown fasting, and is rewarded for killing, or for coming back after an unsuccessful flight. Hence the use of the "lure"—a dead pigeon at the end of a string, or a couple of wings tied together and weighted, and garnished with some raw meat, which is only shown to the hawk at feeding-time, or when she is required to return to her owner, or, again, if she is too far down wind, when the dogs are "standing." As a rule, hawks are fed but once a day, about five o'clock in the afternoon ; but Merlins are all the better for having a light morning meal in addition, about 7 a.m. Indeed, I have found it a good plan to give all hawks a mouthful or two in the morning, after they have got rid of their casting (that is, after they have thrown up the indigestible portion of their food, in the form of an oval pellet), and at the moment of taking them from the "perch" to set them down upon the "block" to bathe. This puts them in good humour, prevents them from "bating" too much, and an hour or two after they have got perfectly dry, they are keen and in good order for flying.

After a hawk has been "called off" to the "lure," at first with a "creance" or long light line attached to the "jesses," and afterwards without it, she has to be "entered" to the particular "quarry" at which she is intended to be flown. This can best be done by previously shooting a partridge, and, while the hawk is on the wing, throwing it out to her in a long line with which she can be checked in case she should attempt to carry the bird away.

When this has been done a few times, the hawk being always allowed time to break into the "quarry" and get a few good mouthfuls before being taken up, she may be flown at a live partridge. And here it should be noted that it is all-important not to disappoint the hawk in her first flight. To avoid this it is a good plan not to unhood her and put her upon the wing until a covey has been found and marked down. The hawk may then be flown, and the falconer, walking towards the spot where the birds have "put in," will be careful not to flush them until he sees that the hawk is well placed, and with her head towards them, so that she may see them the moment they rise. By this plan he will ensure the best chance of success; for if a hawk kills the first time she is flown it will be the making of her. Another piece of advice I would give is, never to run up to a hawk the moment she has killed, but give her time to plume the quarry and break into it, approaching her quietly, and, when near enough, kneeling down with a bit of meat or a partridge wing in the glove, and holding it under her. She will at once seize it, and, stepping on to the glove, may be lifted up gently by aid of the jesses, which must then be firmly held, lest she should attempt to fly. The mischief of "making in" too quickly to a hawk is that it alarms her, and causes her either to carry off the bird she has killed to a distance, or to fly away without it and give some trouble before she is retaken. The fault of "carrying," thus induced by want of care on the part of the falconer, is one that by all means should be guarded against from the beginning.

On taking a hawk up from the quarry she should have a mouthful or two given her by way of reward. The hood being then replaced, she is ready to rest a while before essaying another flight.

Above all things, gentleness with a hawk is a *sine quâ non*, and a light hand in hooding. The bird has then nothing to be afraid of. Instead of being alarmed at the approach of her owner, lest he should rob her of her prey, she comes to regard him as useful in helping her to secure it, allows herself to be lifted up on his glove, feeds before him, and exhibits every sign of confidence and affection.

GROUSE HAWKING.

It is generally supposed that the presence of wild hawks on a grouse moor is incompatible with the existence of a good stock of game, and that to fly trained hawks for the purpose of catching grouse with them is the surest way to drive the latter off the ground.

This idea is altogether erroneous, and can be founded only on theory or mere supposition. No one who has ever seen any grouse hawking, or knows anything at all about it, is of this opinion; and as a brief statement of experience is preferable to a volume of theory, it may be of interest to note some of the conclusions arrived at after several years actual experiment on English and Scotch moors.

In the first place, it may be stated as a fact that grouse (and partridges, too), are not more frightened by the appearance of a trained falcon than they are at the sight of a wild one. On the appearance of either in the air, their natural instinct prompts them to lie close until the danger is past; or, if they are on the wing and a hawk pursues, they will fly their fastest for some distance, and then drop helter-skelter into the first friendly covert that presents itself—amongst bracken, high heather, or loose-scattered boulders, or even into small plantations, though I have only seen this happen with single birds.

In the second place, it may be accepted as a fact that grouse are only *temporarily* frightened by the appearance or pursuit of a hawk, and not permanently scared away as some people imagine. The next day, perhaps the same evening, they are back on the same ground, and ready for another flight. And this is not merely for two or three consecutive days, but every day for a month or six weeks, so long as the weather is favourable for hawking, the hawks being usually flown in the afternoon. Indeed, when all the attendant circumstances are considered, it is reasonable to conclude that grouse must be much more frightened when driven and shot at than when flushed and flown at by a hawk. The large number of birds disturbed at a time during a drive, the noise, the flash of the guns, the smoke, and, above all, the number of pricked birds that get away, and are reminded for some days at least of the ordeal they have gone through, must, on the whole, be far more disquieting to a grouse moor than the finding of a single covey with a brace of good dogs, say six or eight times in the course of an afternoon, and the silent though marvellously rapid flight of a hawk, resulting in the death of a single grouse on each occasion.

But in saying this, I must not be understood to decry grouse-driving. Far from it. It has been my good fortune to take part in many a grouse drive in

England, Wales, and Scotland, and amidst the most wild and beautiful scenery, to admire in others the skill which I have tried to acquire in this most difficult but fascinating of sports. Indeed, I am one of those who think that shooting and hawking are the things to live for, and I would not uphold the one sport at the expense of the other. I have no intention of trying to prove that grouse hawking is preferable to grouse shooting, for I am not unmindful of the adage, *chacun à son gout*. My only desire is to remove some of the misconceptions which evidently exist concerning the less known but equally fascinating pursuit.

For the reasons above stated, I maintain that the prejudice exhibited by owners of grouse moors in objecting to trained hawks being flown on their ground, is unfounded; and the best proof of this lies in the fact that after five years' grouse hawking (between Aug. 12 and say Oct. 12) on the same moor, on which a moderate number of grouse were also shot, a splendid stock of birds was left, to the evident astonishment of those who had predicted otherwise. The owner of the moor was perfectly satisfied, and had no objection to renew the lease for any number of years.

As to the *modus operandi*, it would be difficult to find words too eulogistic of the sport; at the same time it must be understood that it is not one that can be indulged in at a week's notice by any one who has had no previous experience in managing hawks. Those who think that a trained falcon is to be purchased and used with the same ease as a pointer or setter are very much mistaken, as they would discover probably by losing it the first time it was flown. There is more art in training a hawk than there is in breaking a dog, while to attempt to fly an untrained, partly trained, or badly trained hawk is simply to court disappointment and disaster.

The birds used for grouse hawking are Peregrine Falcons. They may be either "eyesses" taken from English or Scottish nests, and "flown at hack," that is, at liberty for some weeks, while being fed daily at some accustomed spot; or they may be "passage-hawks," that is, hawks taken on passage, or migration, in the autumn after they have been preying for themselves for some months. The choice is optional, and in most cases will depend upon the facilities enjoyed for obtaining either.

The old Scottish falconers preferred "eyesses," and could kill with them from two to three hundred head of game in a season. English falconers as a rule prefer the passage hawks, taken the previous autumn and flown in the spring at rooks and crows by way of preparation for the game season. Passage hawks have certainly this to recommend them, that before they are captured they have learnt to catch and kill prey for themselves, whereas "eyesses" have everything to learn. Here again the motto *chacun à son gout* applies, but it is generally admitted that for partridges the best hawks are "eyess tiercels," and for grouse "passage falcons," the heavier game bird requiring the larger and more powerful hawk.

As we are now dealing with grouse, let us suppose,

first, that you know enough about hawking to have killed a partridge or two with an eyess Peregrine; and, secondly, that you have not only secured three or four good passage falcons, but by due preparation have got them thoroughly into condition and good flying order before essaying a flight at a grouse. In the absence of these conditions it would be useless to attempt it. The grouse would fly clean away from the hawk, and the latter, if she had courage enough to pursue without strength enough to stoop and kill, would stand a good chance of continuing a hopeless stern chase, and getting lost, and perhaps shot.

Assuming, however, that all is right on this score, away we go to the moor. The hawks have been put out early on their blocks, and have been bathing and weathering all the morning. They are now hungry and keen to fly. Sitting hooded on the cadge, or oblong square frame used for carrying them out and home, they are taken to the particular part of the moor where you intend to fly. And here it is well to note that the flattest moors are best, not only to enable you to see the end of a flight, but also to lessen the chance of losing a hawk, should she kill out of sight in rough ground, or in some sequestered spot amongst large boulders, where, even with the aid of her bell, she would be difficult to find. This settled to your satisfaction, a falcon is unhooded and cast off. Away she goes in wide circles, at first just over your head, but gradually rising higher and higher, until at length she is a couple of hundred yards high. As soon as she has gained her "pitch," you uncouple your dogs, pointers or setters as the case may be, and away they go over the purple heather, galloping in that untiring fashion which is as wonderful as it is beautiful to see. Suddenly one of them stands, and is instantly backed by the other. Then they begin to draw on; the grouse are still some way ahead. We look for the hawk; there she is waiting on, still at a great height, and perhaps a little too far down wind. You show her the lure, and, obedient as a dog, she comes up overhead, looking wistfully down in expectation of reward. The dogs are again steady on point. Now is the time. We run down to them in line, and flush the birds. The hawk at once sees them, and with vigorous stroke of wing pursues, until, judging her distance most admirably, she falls with headlong stoop at the bird she has selected, and cuts it over amidst a cloud of feathers. It is a marvellous sight. The glorious wild scenery, the purple heather, and the great grey lichen-covered boulders cropping up here and there; the dogs, half hidden by the long heath stalks, and the noble Falcon, "waiting on," above; while below her the falconer and his friends stand delighted, and await the *dénoûment.* A whirr of brown wings, a shout, a deadly stoop, and a fine old cock Grouse lies stone dead amongst the heather from which he has so lately risen. The Falcon like a flash descends upon his prostrate form, and sits there until you approach to take her up, when, like the well trained bird that she is, she steps lightly on to your glove, is petted and caressed, and rewarded with the head of the grouse, being finally re-hooded and set down upon the cadge, that another favourite may take her turn upon the wing,

In this way, let us suppose, you fly each of your hawks twice, and by the time the sun has sunk behind the hills tingeing the heather with an indescribable lovely glow, you are on your way home with three or four brace of grouse slung beneath the cadge, and with feelings of triumph that can be better imagined than described. Just as a keen shot is proud of the dogs which he has broken and taught to "stand," "back," and "down charge," so are you proud of the hawks you have trained to become equally obedient. To witness, amid such picturesque surroundings, the admirable way in which the dogs and hawks will work in concert, each perfectly understanding the other, is a sight not easily to be forgotten.

The sport ended, the hawks are fed up, and placed upon their perches for the night; perchance to dream of more glorious flights, which, weather permitting, you hope to enjoy on the morrow.

Flying trained hawks on a moor does not drive the grouse away. Allusion has been already made to the popular but erroneous idea that grouse hawking ruins a moor for shooting. The fallacy of this notion, however, has been proved over and over again. It is, of course, perfectly true, that while a trained falcon is on the wing, the grouse are alarmed and lie still; if flushed, will scatter in all directions, speedily seeking shelter again, and for the time being they will quit the ground on which they have been found. But this they will do also in the presence of a wild hawk, their natural enemy. Their alarm is but temporary, and the next day, nay, it may be the same afternoon, they are back on their old ground. I have seen this happen over and over again, when grouse hawking with my friend Major Hawkins Fisher in Northumberland.

When the Rev. G. E. Freeman (to whose essays on Falconry, over the signature "Peregrine," readers of the *Field* are so much indebted for instruction) lived at Wild Boar Clough, near Macclesfield, he had permission to fly his hawks at grouse on a neighbouring moor, and for nearly twenty years enjoyed excellent sport with them. He convinced not only his friends, but what was more to his purpose, the owner of the moor (Mr. Philip Brocklehurst, of Swithamley Park), year after year, that no harm was done to the grouse shooting, and there was always a good stock on the ground at the close of the season.

Major Charlton Anne, of Blenkinsopp Castle, Greenhead, Carlisle, an enthusiastic falconer, on reading the chapter here reprinted on grouse hawking when it first appeared in the *Field* of Oct. 31, 1891, wrote as follows:

Allow me most cordially to endorse your remarks as to game not being driven off their ground by hawks. The following facts speak for themselves. About ten days ago (Oct. 16) a young friend of mine came to see me, and I took him on to a small bit of moor close at hand, to show him a flight at a grouse with a falcon. Now, in the centre of this badly-heathered moor, or, rather, bog, for it is little else, there is a patch of about two acres of fairly good heather, which has never once failed us when we wanted to find a grouse for hawking. This time, although, owing to rough weather, we had not flown a hawk on it for above a week, we nearly drew blank; but at the very far end of it a grouse got up, and the falcon, luckily being well placed amongst the clouds, in a few seconds afterwards stooped and killed it. Next day my friend turned up again unexpectedly, and expressed himself so delighted with his previous day's experience, that he prevailed upon me to put the hawk on the wing again over the same patch of heather. This time the hawk had barely got her pitch when up got, not one grouse, but a large pack of 100 or more. The hawk made a capital stoop at one, and, as we ran up to the kill, grouse kept getting up right and left of us. On the third and following day I went up late in the afternoon with the hawk, accompanied by a friend, and found a lot of grouse on the same two acres, flushing as well a tufted duck, a woodcock, and a short-eared owl! I have frequently shot and hawked with Major Fisher on the Riddlehamhope Moors, where I have followed Lady Jane's and Lundy's bells one day and had a grand day's grouse driving the next *over nearly the same ground.* The prejudice against hawking displayed by the majority of shooting men is remarkable, and is only to be explained by their want of practical acquaintance with the sport. I am as fond of the gun as I am of a hawk, and yet I do not find that the one sport interferes with or spoils the other.

Major Hawkins Fisher, writing at the close of the grouse hawking season of 1887, on the moor above referred to, after mentioning the number of grouse killed by the four falcons which he had with him, viz.: Lady Jane, forty-four; Lundy, twenty-nine; Dutch Lady, twenty; and Princess, fifteen, and a snipe, remarked: "The hawks went out altogether twenty-six times, and their best days were: Aug. 20, nine grouse; Sept. 15, four; 16th, four; 17th, five; 19th, six; 20th, eight; 22nd, seven; 23rd, six; 24th, six, and a full snipe." He concluded as follows:

The keeper now quite believes the evidence which his senses daily afford him that the constant flying of trained hawks on a limited area, and on the same parts of that area, does *not* drive grouse off the ground. I see little or no difference in their numbers to what they were at first, nor does the keeper either. He is quite satisfied that the many hundreds of fine grouse which he and I saw there on Oct. 4 cannot have been driven off by the hawks, and fully expects to show good sport here when the "batteries" are manned, and the "driving" commences. So, although long experience forbids me to hope that any words or proof of mine, or anyone else's, will dispel this delusion, I maintain that the use of trained falcons on a moor does not drive off the grouse.

Captain G. Noble, of Jesmond Dene, Newcastle-upon-Tyne, writing on this subject (*The Field*, Nov. 4, 1893), after describing a successful flight at a Curlew (one of the most difficult birds to kill with a trained hawk) observes: "I am glad to add my quota of corroborative evidence as to the fact that hawking does not frighten away game. On a small piece of ground which I took in September I found far more birds on the shooting at the end of the month than there were at the beginning, though we were out (hawking) nearly every day."

Thus the unanimous testimony of experienced falconers is to the effect that both grouse and partridges are far less disturbed from their haunts by hawking than by shooting.

TRAINING THE MERLIN.

THE LADY'S HAWK.

MERLINS, unlike other hawks which build in cliffs and trees, prefer the open moorland, where generally on rising ground, against the side of a hill or some huge grey stone cropping up amongst the purple heather, the nest lies so well concealed that it is only stumbled upon by accident, unless the parent birds are watched in their visits to and fro. It is a pretty sight to view the young Merlins, as they are getting the use of their wings, taking short flights from one big stone to another, or perched with extended wings and tail on some bare and swaying branch of old heather hardly strong enough to support even their light weight. A sharp reiterated cry is heard in the air, and we look up from our place of concealment to see one of the old birds flying towards the nest with something in her foot. The young, in great excitement in anticipation of a meal, betray their whereabouts by their restless movements, when the old one drops a freshly killed Linnet close to one of them, and it is at once seized and plumed. Gradually as they increase in strength and fullness of wing, they take longer flights, and will soon be able to prey for themselves, and leave the neighbourhood of the nest altogether. Then is the time to try and catch one, for my lady has been promised a Merlin, and a Merlin she must have, if we would not for ever forfeit her good graces by disappointing her. So the well-instructed keeper prepares and sets the fatal snare which is to hold firmly but gently, and quite painlessly, the coveted prize, until he can release and carry it home.*

Then comes the operation of putting on the "jesses," two little narrow straps made out of an old dogskin glove, and fastened one round each leg just above the foot. A slit at the end of each strap enables one to attach the leash (a porpoise-hide bootlace will do) by a tiny swivel, and the little hawk (the smallest which this country produces) is ready to be carried on the glove and gradually tamed and trained. Here the use of the hood comes in, and materially helps the trainer, for the bird sits quietly when hooded, and allows itself to be handled and gently stroked, until at length it loses all fear of man, and will jump from the perch to the glove twice a day to be fed, the distance being judiciously increased until at length a short flight is necessary to reach the proffered meat.

The question of food is an all-important one with Merlins: their delicate organisation cannot brook the ordinary lean beef or tough heads and necks of fowls that larger hawks can dispose of; they must have something lighter, less fibrous, and more easily digestible. Experience has proved that there is

* An illustration of the snare used will be found further on in the chapter on "Devices for Taking Hawks."

nothing better than a bit of sheep's heart in the morning, and a small bird with the feathers on in the evening.

On no account must the small bird be offered in the morning, for, since it is the practice of all birds of prey, some hours after feeding, to cast up and eject, in pellet form, the feathers and other indigestible portions of their food, these should only

FIG. 20.—THE MERLIN.

be administered at the evening meal, that the hawk may have the whole night to carry out the peculiar digestive process which Nature has ordained. To give a Merlin a full crop of sheep's heart after breakfasting upon a small bird, and before the "casting" has been thrown up, would cause a serious attack of indigestion, which might perhaps prove fatal.

If the little hawk is not to be "flown at hack," that is, allowed its liberty round about the place where it is daily fed (an excellent plan where the safety of the bird can be insured), it must be "called off" to the "lure" morning and evening. That is to say, a light line (technically called a "creance") must be attached to the ends of the "jesses," and the trainer, standing a few yards off with a "lure," made of a bunch of feathers weighted, and garnished with food (see Fig. 15), must swing the "lure," and call the bird off the hand of an assistant (or off a post or gate), repeating the process until it has been well exercised, and rewarding it for coming every time with a mouthful or two of meat, which it will keenly devour, for it must be flown fasting. Gradually the length of the flight is increased, and as soon as the hawk comes well to the "lure," the line or "creance" is dispensed with, and the bird is allowed to remain a little time on the wing by snatching away the lure as it is on the point of being seized. The hawk dashes by, looking for the "lure," and returns on being shown it again. In this way the daily exercise is increased, the hawk gets strong on the wing and sound in wind, until finally it may be entered at the "quarry" it is destined to be flown at. For this purpose it is desirable to procure some small bird (a lively sparrow will do), which should be flown in a string, and the hawk allowed to pursue and kill it. It has been found a good plan to fasten one end of the "creance" to the hawk and the other end to the live "quarry," which not only ensures a reward to the hawk, which should not be disappointed, but enables the trainer who follows the flight to tread upon the line on approaching the hawk, and so prevent it from carrying the quarry away, which it will very likely try to do the first time, imagining that the trainer is approaching to rob it of its prey. It is most important to let the hawk discover that this is not the case, and allow it to kill, plume, and begin to feed before it is taken up on the glove, where it should be allowed to finish its meal. In this way it gains confidence, and soon acquires affection for its owner, whom it learns to regard as a helpmate in the chase. And here it may be remarked, in anticipation of any charge of cruelty, that there can be nothing cruel in training a hawk to do for our pleasure what it has to do every day of its life in a state of nature in order to live. It is no more cruel to the small bird to be killed by a tame hawk than by a wild one; the mode of death is the same—quick, and often painless, for a sudden dislocation of the neck paralyses it, and death is almost instantaneous.

The pleasure of hawking arises when the Merlin, first trained by means of an ignoble Sparrow, is flown at a mounting Lark. Then, indeed, is there an aerial chase well worth witnessing. The Lark, relying upon its power of wing, springs up with a defiant twitter, as if to say, "catch me if you can," and quickly attains a good height. The Merlin, flying into the wind, ascends in spiral curves, getting higher and higher at every turn, until at length she is above the Lark, which often does not wait for the fatal "stoop," but drops to earth like a stone, and hides in the nearest covert at hand. But "how cruel" the reader may perhaps exclaim, "to fly your hawk at a lark; of all birds, why a lark, that sings so beautifully," &c., &c. The lark is chosen for his mounting qualities, and strong and sustained flight, which really test the powers of a hawk. With a sparrow, linnet, or other small bird there would be no flight at all; it would be caught immediately. The very essence of the sport is the aerial contest which takes place between two well-matched birds. Then, as to the supposed cruelty, it is not more cruel to kill a lark than a sparrow, especially when it is remembered that lark-hawking does not commence until after the nesting season is over; when the birds have no longer any eggs or young to care for, when they are beginning to flock before migrating for the winter, and when hundreds of others are about to visit us and take their place from countries further north. Larks are netted wholesale for expectant poulterers, who have no difficulty in disposing of them to those who, having admired their song in spring, have no objection to eat them in the winter. Why, then, should there be any sentiment about taking toll of a few with a well-trained Merlin?

But all this time my lady is anxiously awaiting the arrival of the promised hawk. She has found, upon the bookshelves in an old country house, Turbervile's "Booke of Falconrie," dated 1575, and the "Falcon's Lure and Cure," by Symon Latham, 1615, in which she has lost no time in discovering the pages which treat of the Merlin, and is delighted to read the Elizabethan falconer's praise of these little hawks. "Assuredly," he says, "divers of these Merlyns become passing good hawkes, and verie skilfull. Their property by nature is to kill Thrushes, Larks, and Partridges. They flee with greater fiercenes and more hotely than any other hawke of prey."*

And now her anxiety is how to get the Merlin safely from the keeper without breaking any flight feathers. In the olden time a hawk was sent by hand, or, if several were to be forwarded, they travelled on a "cadge," or wooden frame, supported by leathern straps across a man's shoulders. They were obliged to be carried in those days, for they had to be fed on the way. Now long journeys can be so quickly accomplished by rail, that a hawk may be trusted to travel alone if properly packed. It is only necessary to secure a roomy hamper, and to line both the inside and the lid, but not the bottom, with stout calico, wrappering, or cheese cloth, which is stitched in top and bottom, and effectually prevents the hawk from breaking her wing feathers or injuring herself by jumping against the roof in her efforts to get out. The tail feathers sometimes get a little bent or broken, the risk of which may be lessened by tying two pieces of wood crosswise on the bottom of the basket, to form a perch that may be well grasped by the bird to steady herself in case

* An old French falconer, Nicholas Bonnefous, writing in 1681, says a Merlin should be trained in eight days or it is not worth having. "Il doit estre oyselé en huit jours, autrement il ne vaut rien."—*Traité de Fauconnerie*, p. 50.

of a sudden lurch. Should any of the feathers, nevertheless, become bent or bruised, they may be straightened by holding them in boiling water (the hawk being hooded), and pinching them into their proper direction. On opening the hamper on its arrival, care should be taken to get hold of the ends of the jesses with the gloved hand before the bird is lifted out, and the risk of its escape may be lessened by doing this in a room with doors and windows closed. The hawk should then be placed upon the perch, previously prepared, to which it is fastened by means of the leash, while a broad strip of sack-cloth, nailed along the under side of the perch, and allowed to drop below it, will prevent the hawk from swinging should she "bate off," and enable her without much trouble to regain the perch, a feat which she would never accomplish if the so-called "curtain" were absent.

And now, my lady being at length happy in the possession of a hawk, we will leave her to feed it on her glove, and replace it on the perch for the night, reserving for another chapter some practical directions for its proper management in the field.

(*To be continued.*)

LARK HAWKING WITH MERLINS.

In the last chapter an attempt was made to revive the interest which ladies formerly took in the old pastime of hawking, to show how much enjoyment may be derived from the pursuit, and to explain briefly the initial stages of taming and training which are necessary to be gone through before the hawk can be flown at wild quarry. We have seen how the hawk is to be procured and forwarded without injury; furnished with hood, jesses, swivel, and leash; fed upon the gloved hand of the owner, and properly tied upon its perch. The form and appearance of the perch will be best understood by glancing at the illustration on p. 7. From this it will be seen that the perch is a slender pole supported on two uprights, and covered with stout canvas or drugget, with a curtain also of canvas depending from the under side, and strained at the bottom to keep it steady, the object being to prevent the hawk from swinging backwards and forwards, as it would otherwise do if it were to "bate off"—that is, fly suddenly off the perch and hang head downwards by its leash. This canvas "curtain" enables the bird to recover itself, turn round, and regain the perch without damage to the wings or tail, which it is most important to preserve unbroken.*

Before being set upon the perch, the hawk should be fed upon the owner's gloved hand, and here it may be observed that the best food for a Merlin (the lady's hawk) is sheep's heart, which is less fibrous and more easily digested than any other butcher's meat—in this respect approximating to the flesh of small birds, upon which the hawk habitually feeds. But in order to keep the Merlin in health, it should not be confined to a diet of sheep's heart, but be fed in the evening of every second or third day with a sparrow, lark, or any other small bird that can be most easily procured, it being important that the hawk should swallow a certain amount of feathers (or mouse's fur will answer the purpose) to cleanse the stomach, or "panel," as a falconer would say, and keep the bird in health.

For this purpose, also, a bath every second or third day is very desirable, and is much enjoyed by the hawk. To administer this properly, the bird should be set down upon a "block" on the lawn, close to which the bath (a shallow zinc tray, holding water to the depth of about 2 inches) should be previously placed. In this case, of course, the hawk's tether will be nearly the length of the leash, the end of which is tied to a ring in the block, the button end preventing it from slipping through the ring of the swivel. Just before bathing, in the morning, a few mouthfuls of sheep's heart may be

* See the remarks on this subject, and the proper mode of setting down a hawk on the perch (pp. 8-9).

given, and after the bath the hawk will sit on the block until dry. In the afternoon, about two or three o'clock, she will be ready to fly, and then begins the real sport. But it is important to observe that on no account must the hawk be flown loose—that is, without a line (or "creance," as it is termed) to the swivel—*until she will come well to the hand with it on*, and fly well to the "lure" (already described and figured, p. 39) when the latter is thrown to a distance with the right hand.

The next stage is to "enter" the hawk at live "quarry," a small bird in a string some twenty or thirty yards long, and when this is eagerly taken, she is ready for the field. We will now suppose that the hawk, lightly fed in the morning, bathed, and "weathered" on her block, is carried out in the afternoon on her owner's glove, ready for a flight. The more open the country and the larger the field selected the better, while the ground to be chosen should be that whereon larks are most likely to be found. No eyess Merlin should be trained to anything else but larks. These afford sport more nearly resembling heron-hawking than any other quarry; and the young Merlins will take these well throughout August and most of September while they are still in moult. Detaching the leash and swivel, my lady will proceed to walk up wind, holding the ends of the jesses tightly between the forefinger and thumb to prevent the hawk "bating off" and getting away before the proper time. A Lark is flushed, and if at a distance, is marked down to insure the certainty of a flight; when, walking straight to the spot, the

Lark again rises, and the Merlin is instantly cast off. Then ensues an aerial chase, perchance into the clouds, which will reward the owner for all the trouble that has been bestowed, and excite the most lively feelings of wonderment and delight at the marvellous powers of flight displayed both by pursuer and pursued. Following every twist and turn of the Lark, the Merlin at length forces its "quarry" to take the air, when both birds ring up, each striving to get above the other. Sometimes the Lark proves too good, and escapes altogether; sometimes, on seeing the hawk above, it descends to the ground like a stone, and is captured. Frequently it takes refuge in a hedge, ditch, or bush; often in a field of standing corn; wherever, in fact, it can find shelter enough to hide it.

To recover the hawk, whether she has killed or not, requires a little care and judgment. Should she be found with the Lark in her foot, she must not be approached too hastily, or she will "carry"—that is, fly away with the quarry, a most troublesome habit, and difficult to cure if once contracted. On nearing the spot where she has come down, the falconer will pause to look about until the Merlin can be seen, and is allowed to "break into" her quarry, which is now dead. Approaching gently, the owner will stoop down, and presenting the lure, on which a bit of sheep's heart has been tied, or simply holding a bit in the gloved hand, will present it to the hawk, who, having been flown fasting, is eager to feed, and will soon step up on to the glove to continue the meal as usual. But this must not be permitted; a mouthful or two is all that can be allowed if the hawk is to be flown again that day, and this she assuredly should be, for the more flying she can get the better she will become.

Should the Merlin fail to take the Lark, and perch on the top of a hedge or in a tree, or remain flying round and round, the "lure" must be swung and thrown out on an open spot where the hawk can see it well, when she will fly down to it, and, after being allowed a mouthful of the meat with which it is garnished, may be taken up gently on the glove as before (the "lure" being at once pocketed), and carried in search of another Lark.

After the last flight (three or four will generally suffice), she may be fed up, carried home unhooded, and tied upon the perch for the night.

There are many little "dodges" in connection with falconry which can be learnt only by experience, or the personal teaching of a practised hand; and the management of different kinds of hawk is not always alike. But it is hoped that enough has been said to show that hawking is a delightful field sport in which ladies may gracefully and cleverly take part, and that it is neither so difficult nor so fatiguing as other forms of exercise in which many ladies at the present day have learnt to excel.

Lark Hawking on Salisbury Plain.

The following account of Lark-hawking with Merlins on Salisbury Plain, furnished by Mr. E. B.

Michell, who has been most successful in training these little hawks, will convey a good idea of the sport which may be obtained with them if properly managed :

I send you the short results of ten days' lark-hawking on the Plain with four of the most unmanageable eyess Merlins I have ever had the luck to train. As one or other of these hawks was often lost, the flights were not very numerous, and the weather was anything but favourable—so hot at first that hawks could not well be flown, except before eight and after five; and afterwards very windy, wet, and changeable. The Merlins were flown partly in single flights and partly double, some of the double ones being flown in company with the Merlins of a friend, who, during a part of the time, brought two of them to the same place. As it is difficult to apportion the credit due to each hawk in a double flight, I have kept these separate from the others, and scored them somewhat differently, marking a miss only when the lark escaped, and it was clear that neither hawk was entitled to the honours of victory. So arranged, the score-sheet reads thus:

SINGLE FLIGHTS.

	Flights.	Kills.	Beaten off.
Undine (female)	23	20	0
Ladymead (female)	15	9	3
Diamond (male)	16	12	1
Blue Ribbon (male)	15	8	3

Total: 69 flights, 49 kills.

DOUBLE FLIGHTS (TWO HAWKS TOGETHER).

	Flights.	Successful.	Unsuccessful.
Undine	3	2	1
Ladymead	8	7	1
Diamond	13	12	1
Blue Ribbon	14	11	3

Total: 38 flights, 32 kills.

Grand total: 88 larks flown, 65 taken, 15 escaped into covert, and 8 beat the hawks fairly in the air.

This score is no doubt exceptionally good; but it must be observed that the country chosen was perhaps the best in England; that the best part of the day was utilised, some flights having been flown before 7 a.m., and others after 7 p.m., when the wind was least troublesome; that the hawks had had some previous flying in another tolerable country; and, finally, that the larks are now (Sept. 1) deep in moult. Late-bred larks, not yet strong on the wing, afford very poor flights, and greatly spoil the sport. On the other hand, many old larks seem to fly as well as if they were fully moulted, and take the air singing notes of cheery defiance, as they do in November. Very few of the weak larks fell to the lot of Undine, who had the lion's share of hard flights, and was therefore in the best condition. No lark on the Plain ever beat her off—that is to say, kept the air till she abandoned the pursuit. Twice she brought down her lark from a height when he was out of sight, and killed him after more than eighteen stoops. Nine Larks in succession she killed without a miss. Diamond went up after one lark till both he and the lark were out of sight above in a clear sky. Once, when flying with a well-trained and plucky female Merlin (Beauty), he had two stoops at a ringing lark, a quarter of a mile high, before the other could get one, and afterwards footed the lark, which I saved alive, the little hawk being too "blown" to kill it before I came up.

On the whole, having had a good opportunity of comparing males with females, I am of opinion that the difference between them, for lark flying, is not very great. A really good male, like Diamond, is decidedly better than a moderate female, like Ladymead. The larks, however, dread a female Merlin more than a male, from which it may be inferred that in the wild state the former is superior in powers of mounting. In conclusion, I may add that, in order to achieve such results as the above, Merlins must be kept as fat and strong as wild hawks.

Lark Hawking in an enclosed Country.

By way of contrast to the sport obtainable in the open plain, Capt. C. H. Thompson, writing from Charminster, Sept. 22, 1890, gives the following illustration of what may be done with Merlins in an enclosed country:

I send you an account of a short season with a cast of Merlins which I obtained when fully "hacked" and in beautiful condition the end of July. Unfortunately, the rough and wet weather of August postponed the opening day till the 23rd of that month, the 12th being what I consider the usual opening day. From Aug. 23 to Sept. 12 my bag was 42 Larks, 1 various. The season included actually sixteen days when I was out with the Merlins; but of these eight were either so rough and rainy that I could only get a flight between the storms, or else were days when I went out for an hour either before or after shooting, and can scarcely be called "full" days, as the little hawks on these eight days rarely had more than one flight apiece. The total for these eight days was 12 larks, 1 various, thus leaving 30 larks for the remaining eight days, when I was out either all the morning or all the afternoon. Of the total bag, "Jack" killed 13 larks, while "Jill" is credited with 29 larks, 1 various.

I give the above full details to show what can be done in an enclosed country, where the fields are generally only a few acres in extent, and, moreover, are bounded by high hedges, with often wide ditches covered with brambles and long grass, which affords excellent covert for the larks to drop into. When in good fettle "Jill" would never give up, and would follow the lark up, up, up, climbing the skies in huge spirals, often chattering and screeching the while from pure light-heartedness, until at last she got above her quarry, when both would drop like stones to the nearest hedge, the brave, fearless little "Jill" dashing through the thickest brambles, and rarely missing her quarry. Often I have had the greatest difficulty in getting at hawk and quarry, and have had to cut away a regular hole before I could reach them, the marvel being to me how the hawk ever got through. Another description of flight is an end-on stern chase, when the fearful lark seeks shelter in the nearest hedge. My best day with these two hawks was six flights and six kills in one afternoon. Latterly I used to let a spaniel—useless for shooting—hunt the stubbles in front of me, for it is wonderful how, after a few flights over a field, the larks lie, and positively refuse to get up unless one almost treads on them. I may add that I never slipped either of the Merlins until they had just "roused." Immediately they had done that I knew they were fit for another flight, and, moreover, would fly well and do their best. I invariably kept them very highly fed, their daily ration, when procurable, being two fresh larks apiece.

THE HOBBY AND BARBARY FALCON.

HE who has chanced to come into possession of a young Hobby may congratulate himself upon being the owner of, perhaps, the swiftest hawk that flies. There is no reason why Hobbies should not take moulted Larks—a feat which has never been accomplished with any permanent success by Merlins. The only fault of the Hobby is want of perseverance, and this, no doubt, arises in a great measure from its insectivorous habits in a state of nature, its food consisting largely of beetles, crane-flies, dragon-flies, and other winged insects, in pursuit of which it may be seen making graceful evolutions in the air. No hawk is more easily trained, and none flies more beautifully to the lure. He may be kept on the wing for a very long time, and allowed to rake away to a great distance, when a wave of the lure will bring him up from a mile off with lightning speed. But with all his splendid powers of flight, the Hobby, like the Kestrel, is a lazy and unpersevering bird. He seems to want pluck, and after ringing up in good style after a mounting lark, and looking as if he was sure to kill, he will give up the chase and turn idly away down wind as if it were beneath his dignity to take more trouble. It is very doubtful how far this disposition was overcome by the old falconers, or what were the real performances of what they termed "the young man's hawk." But whoever hopes for success with him nowadays must be careful never to let his bird have an easy time of it. No bagged quarry should be employed, and if he should be induced to take a moulting lark in August, he should be allowed to eat and enjoy it. He must not be managed like a Merlin, but like a Peregrine, which means that one meal a day is sufficient, and that to be earned by a good bout of "waiting on," and stooping at the lure.

Some years ago, in company with a friend, in Essex (Mr. Brewster), who sometimes secured a nest of young Hobbies in his neighbourhood, we had some very pretty flights at larks on the cleared stubbles and big grass fields, and the greater speed of the Hobby as compared with that of the Merlin was remarkable. Of the two, the Hobby has a much longer wing, and looks more like a large Swift when flying. The late Lord Lilford tried the experiment of flying some young Hobbies "at hack" (*Zoologist*, 1886, p. 469), but, on taking them up, they began to droop one after another, so they were turned adrift again. They remained about the park for a short time, but all took their departure before the middle of September. Mr. E. B. Michell had an excellent Hobby, some years ago, which afforded a rare treat to those who saw it fly on the downs at Epsom, where at various times we have flown the Peregrine, Jerfalcon, Merlin, Lanner, and Barbary Falcon. A cast of the last named beautiful little hawks, obtained through Mr. Philip Castang, of Leadenhall Market, flew to perfection "to the lure," at a swing of which the tiercel would descend out of the sky straight on to the outstretched arm, as if alighting on the branch of a tree, and both were so tame that for some weeks in August, in order to prepare them

FIG. 21.—THE HOBBY.

for partridge-hawking, they were flown "to the lure" every afternoon in Hyde Park, as many friends of the writer can testify. General Griffiths, an experienced Anglo-Indian falconer, who saw them flying thus in the middle of London, was astonished at their docility, and obedience to the lure. Shortly afterwards on going northwards for grouse-hawking with my old friend Major C. H. Fisher, I took the Barbary Falcons with me, but finding no partridges on the moor, and grouse being too strong and heavy for them, we flew them at pigeons liberated on the open moor at a distance from home, putting both of them on the wing at once, and allowing them to ring up well before tossing a pigeon to them. In this way we had many pretty flights and excellent stooping. Afterwards I took them for partridge-hawking into Rutlandshire, where one of them was unfortunately lost by chasing a wood-pigeon, which decoyed him away down wind and out of sight. Nor was he heard of again. The other was given to a friend in Yorkshire in exchange for a Peregrine tiercel.

I agree with the authors of "Falconry in the British Isles" in regarding the Barbary Falcon (which in colour and markings resembles a miniature Peregrine) as the *beau ideal* of what a falcon should be—a model of strength and speed combined.

The few young Lanners which I have procured from Mogador, through Mr. Castang, and trained at different times (though not of late years) all seemed to me dull and spiritless compared with the Barbary Falcon, which with proper management should make a perfect hawk for partridges.

In former days, however, the Lanner appears to have been flown by English falconers with considerable success, to judge by the account given of it by Simon Latham.*

---

* See "Latham's Falconry," Second Book (1618), p. 112.

TRAINING THE SPARROW-HAWK.

MANY people seem to be under an impression that because the Sparrow-hawk is one of the easiest hawks to procure, it is therefore the best for a would-be falconer to begin with. This, however, is not the case. As will presently appear, there are many reasons why a Merlin is to be preferred; but if the latter is not to be obtained when wanted, the former may be taken in hand *faute de mieux*.

The young of the two species may be readily distinguished by the following characters, independently of the colour of the plumage.

The Merlin has long, pointed wings, comparatively short legs and toes, and a dark brown eye with a black pupil; the Sparrow-hawk has short rounded wings, long thin legs and toes, and a light coloured eye, at first pale greenish or yellowish grey, then pale yellow, and finally, in the adult, bright yellow with a black pupil. It is well to remember that the young birds should never be taken in a helpless condition from the nest, in which case they will not only give more trouble, but will never be so good as when taken at a later period of their existence, and, from their habit of constantly clamouring for food, are almost certain to become confirmed "screamers," a detestable fault in the eyes of a falconer.

The nest should be watched daily until the young birds are able to leave it, and may be seen perched upon the edge of it or on branches close by, when, in the language of falconry, they are known as "branchers" or "ramage-hawks." In this condition they are only just able to use their wings to steady themselves, and cannot fly far. This is the time then to secure them. By sending a boy up the tree with a ball of string in his pocket, by means of which he may afterwards draw up a long thin wand, he may drive them from branch to branch till they fall fluttering down to the hands of their captor. Or if the birds be perched not too high up they may be reached with a noose at the end of a fishing rod. Should it happen, however, that they have left the nest sometime before they are discovered, and are fairly strong on the wing, they may be snared in one of the ways described further on in the chapter headed "Devices for Taking Hawks."

Let us suppose, then, that the captor is in a position to select from three or four birds caught at the proper time, he will make a great mistake in trying to keep them all. He should select no more than two, choosing the largest and heaviest with the best legs and feet. These will probably be females, and will be best adapted for the purpose in view, for with birds of prey the females are always larger and more powerful than the males. The first thing to do on securing one is to put the jesses on the legs, while an assistant holds the bird firmly but gently with the wings pressed close against the sides. The shape of the jesses (which may be made of strips cut out of an old dogskin glove), and the mode of fastening them has been already described with an illustration (see p. 23).

They are, of course, narrower for a Sparrow-hawk than for a Falcon, and provided the dogskin is

Fig. 22.—The Sparrow-Hawk

sound, of equal thickness throughout, and well greased, they may be as narrow as is consistent with strength. The use of a swivel and leash is not necessary at first, for it is better to give the birds their liberty for some time in an outhouse until they have gained strength and got accustomed to feed on the hand. The outhouse should be as empty as possible. It will never do to have a lot of loose boxes or hampers lying about behind which the birds may creep and hide and give much trouble before they can be discovered, to say nothing of the risk they would run from the attacks of rats amongst such rubbish. It goes without saying that having cleared the place, all rat holes should be carefully stopped. A single shelf may be put up on which to stand a low, strong, and heavy basket without a lid, and with a good thick rim, such as the fruiterers use for a bushel of potatoes or other vegetables. This will never be displaced by the birds' weight, and the stout rim will form a most convenient roosting place. Across the angles of the room may be fixed perches, about as high as one may reach with outstretched hand, so that a hawk may fly from one to another, and, if need be, can be lifted down by the jesses without the use of a ladder. All this being in readiness, the birds, after being fed, should be placed on the basket and left quiet until the time arrives for the next meal.

As to feeding, it is important to bear in mind that young hawks require food oftener than old ones. A falcon, when trained, is fed but once a day, but a young hawk while growing should be fed night and morning. With all birds of prey the digestion is very rapid, and as the food is received into the crop, the quantity to be given may be regulated by the visible swelling of the crop. The old falconers all say "Beware of great gorges," and they are quite right. Overfeeding will prove fatal. For a young Sparrow-hawk, a meal should at first not exceed in bulk the size of a partridge or grouse egg, and care should be taken not to give any "casting" (fur or feathers) with the morning meal. Even at the twilight meal the "casting" should be very light with young birds, for they should be brought up as naturally as possible, and we have to remember that so long as they are in the nest, and until they are able to prey for themselves, they are fed by their parents in mouthfuls, and receive much less "casting" than they subsequently get when able to break up quarry for themselves. For choice, there is nothing better than mice and sparrows, so long as they can be procured, but failing these, the butcher should be asked to send a fresh sheep's heart every day at a cost of fourpence. Beef or mutton will not do for a Sparrow-hawk or a Merlin; it is too tough and fibrous, and will prove fatal if continued, although upon an emergency a bit of lean beef may be given, if beaten tender, and scored across and across to ensure its being easily pulled to pieces. But sheep's heart approximates more than anything else to the natural food obtained by hawks. It is easily broken up and easily digested. Care must of course be taken not to give with it any of the fat or skin by which it is surrounded.

The housing and the feeding having been now considered, we may proceed to the handling and training.

The hawk should never have her food thrown down to her, as one would throw a bone to a dog. It should be presented to her as she sits upon her perch, and as soon as she has seized it with her foot, and pulled a mouthful or two, she should be lifted gently by means of the jesses on to the gloved hand, and encouraged to finish her meal there. By degrees she will hardly wait for the meat to be offered to her, but will come off the perch of her own accord, and alight on the glove with evident signs of expectation and pleasure. In this she should be encouraged as much as possible, and while she is feeding, her owner should stroke her on the head and down the back with the wing of some small bird. She will resent this at first, and open her wings as if about to fly, but by degrees she will get accustomed to it, and will eventually allow herself to be handled without showing the slightest fear.

The distance she has to come from the perch to the hand must be increased a little every day, until at length she will fly right across the room. Every time she alights upon the glove she must be held there by the jesses and carried about while she feeds, not ravenously, but a little bit at a time. The more she is carried about bareheaded (that is without a hood), and accustomed to the sight of people passing, horses, dogs, and so forth, the better, as she will gradually learn to lose fear of them, and when eventually trained and flown, will come back to her owner boldly.

This carrying of the hawk is the most troublesome part of the training, for the Sparrow-hawk is much more given to bate off the fist than a Merlin or Falcon, and at first, in her endeavours to fly away, will be perpetually hanging head downwards and fluttering in a way most vexatious to a beginner. There is nothing for it but to lift her with the right hand gently on to the glove again, and remain still for a minute or so until she recovers her composure. This will happen over and over again, until the owner feels almost inclined to give up the task as hopeless; and his discomfiture will be increased by the paroxysms of cramp to which Sparrow-hawks are very liable, causing them to extend the legs rigidly, and exhibit a loss of power to grasp the glove and sit upright. Perseverance, however, and gentleness will prevail, and sooner or later the bird will give up "bating," and become less nervous.

When this desirable state of things has been reached, another step in the training may be taken. A light line may be fastened to the loops of the jesses, and the bird may be set upon a field gate and "called off" some twenty or thirty yards, the owner holding the other end of the line in case of accident. When a Hawk will come well to the glove in this way, a sparrow, or other small bird, may be flown in another line, and the hawk encouraged to pursue and capture it, care being taken, of course, to fly her when she is hungry, and therefore keen. When she has seized the quarry, the falconer should be in no hurry to rush up to her. She should be allowed to kill it, and commence feeding before she is gently lifted up to finish her meal on the glove. This part of the programme should be repeated every day at the evening flight, until it is evident that the line may be dispensed with, and the hawk may be flown free. After she has killed a few times, she will acquire confidence in her own powers, and may then be tried at wild quarry, such as a Thrush, for instance, rising out of a turnip field and going well away across the field, at a sufficient distance from the hedgerow to give the hawk time to overtake and kill it. After a few such flights as this, the hawk is "made," and then the more she is flown the better she becomes.

There are, of course, many things to be observed in the training of a hawk which can only be learned by experience, but the following hints will be useful. Never fly a hawk in a high wind, or after rain when the roots are wet. Never fly her at quarry which is too strong and heavy for her, such as an old partridge or a wood-pigeon. Blackbirds and thrushes, of which there are always plenty in the roots in autumn, will afford excellent sport, with an occasional landrail out of clover, or a water-hen by the brookside. Thrushes are migratory in autumn; and the falconer need never have misgiving about killing them at this season of the year. Those which his hawk does not get will pass on, and he will never see them again.

As to water-hens, the plan is to find one out feeding some thirty or forty yards from the brook, the further away the better. Then, keeping close to the water's edge until exactly opposite it, walk straight towards it. For a few seconds it will crouch down, expecting to escape detection, but finding this hopeless, it will rise and fly, right or left, in a semi-circle towards the water. This is the time to slip the hawk, which will then cut off its retreat and take it well out in the open.

FIG. 23.—THE SPARROW-HAWK IN FLIGHT.

(From Oswald Crawfurd's "Year of Sport.")

When your hawk has killed, never run up in a hurry; give her time to break into the quarry.

Never approach her from behind; let her see you coming, and approach slowly. Go down quietly on one knee, and offer her a little bit of meat on the glove. Let her swallow it, and offer a larger piece, holding it tight, when she will put her foot on it in an attempt to seize it. The ends of the jesses should then be taken hold of, and by these the bird is lifted up on the glove.

After a flight the hawk should not be allowed to eat much, that is if she is to be flown again. Her keenness will be in proportion to her unsatisfied appetite. Just a mouthful or two by way of reward and encouragement is all that is needed, and, after a rest, you may look out for some fresh quarry. After the last flight of the day the hawk may be allowed to "feed up" on what she has killed, and should then be carried home, and set down on her perch to be left quiet for the night.

The next morning a search should be made under the perch for the oval-shaped "pellet" or "casting," which envelops the indigestible portions of the food, and is generally thrown up at dawn. Until this is got rid of, the hawk will not be ready to take any more food, and should be allowed to remain undisturbed. Of course, if no fur or feathers have been taken overnight with the food, there will be no "casting" to look for in the morning.

By way of encouragement to beginners, and to show what sport may be had with Sparrow-hawks, I may quote from a letter received from Mr. John Riley, of Putley Court, Herefordshire, who, living in an enclosed country, cannot fly falcons without risk of losing them. He writes: "I had the best Sparrow-hawk last season that I ever possessed. With her I took 1 Pheasant (three parts grown), 3 Partridges, 56 Blackbirds, 5 Thrushes, 2 small birds, and 4 Waterhens; total, 71 head. My next best hawk took 44 Blackbirds, 13 Thrushes, 1 Partridge, and 2 small birds; total, 60 head. Both these hawks were eyesses."

It will be observed that the foregoing directions have reference chiefly to the bringing up and training of "eyesses," *i.e.*, young birds taken from the nest, or (preferably) soon after they have left it.

Something should now be said of the "haggard," or wild caught adult bird.

Just as a passage falcon is superior to an eyess, having been on the wing for some time, and having learnt to catch and kill prey for herself, so is a haggard Sparrow-hawk to be preferred to an eyess, being as easily trained, knowing her business from the start, and giving less trouble in feeding.* All that is needed is "carrying." The old falconers used to say that a hawk should know no perch but her master's fist, and certainly the more a Sparrow-hawk is carried by her owner the more docile and tractable will she become.

The following observations by Mr. E. B. Michell on the training of Sparrow-hawks are so much to the

---

* The female Sparrow-hawk is to be preferred to the male, or "musket," as it was called of old, on account of her greater size and strength.

point that, at the risk of some little repetition, they may well be quoted here:

Although it is tolerably easy to get Sparrow-hawks, either young or old, there seem to be very few men indeed who will take the trouble to train and fly them. This is a mistake; for in the hands of a man who has a fair stock of patience the Sparrow-hawk is one of the most serviceable and deadly birds a falconer can keep. She may be flown in a comparatively enclosed country, at a great variety of quarry—which can easily be found—and will afford, even single-handed, a capital afternoon's sport. Moreover, as she can carry a bell, there is much less chance of losing her than a Merlin or a male Hobby. The great obstacle which hinders men from keeping Sparrow-hawks is the difficulty of training them. It is the exception when one is found which can be managed easily from the first—such as the storied Sparrow-hawk with which Sir John Sebright killed a partridge ten days after she had been caught. Occasionally a hawk of this kind, if it falls at once into good hands, becomes obedient in a very short time; but the beginner must be prepared to exercise a large amount of patience and good-temper in vanquishing the combined shyness, irritability, and obstinacy of his patient. These innate vices of character, though rare in the nobler falcon, and almost unknown in the case of eyess Peregrines and Merlins, are seldom absent from nestling Sparrow-hawks, which are, if possible, still more troublesome and refractory than the adults. They can only be overcome by constant "carrying," and by observing the greatest care never to frighten the hawk. Another very important matter is the dieting, which for this, as for every other description of small hawk, should be plentiful but light. Sparrow-hawks should have very light and digestible meat—either small birds, which are by far the best thing for them, being the natural and habitual food of the species, or extremely tender beef, chopped so that it can be easily eaten, with a frequent change to such softer substance as sheep's heart, and occasionally a mouse. All Sparrow-hawks, and more especially males, should be fed at least twice a day, not only because one crop, however full, is insufficient for them, but because by giving the food in two instalments, say half a crop at one time and three-quarters of a crop at another, the digestion is not overtaxed, and the hawk is never reduced to that torpid state caused by a gorge. Moreover, by this practice the falconer can fly his hawks twice a day, and if he is kept at home by the weather in the morning, can feed them moderately and reserve them for a possible chance in the afternoon.

Throughout the time when the Sparrow-hawk, after being taken up from hack, is being trained, her tail should be kept tied up, as its long feathers are so apt to get bent and broken in "bating." But there is a right and a wrong way of tying the tail, as there is of doing most things required in the falconer's art. The best way is to take a piece of strong thread, and tie it in a single knot round the shaft of the outer feather on one side about half-way down it. One end should then be passed *under* the tail and the other *over* it, the two reuniting and being tied round the shaft of the outer feather on the other side, at a like distance from its extremity, taking care that the thread encircles only the shaft without enclosing any of the web. If the hawk is annoyed by the restraint, and begins to pick and pull at the threads, they will soon slip off and set the tail free. A hawk in pluming herself always passes her beak down the feathers from base to tip, and as there is no tight knot on either of the feathers round which the threads pass, they can be slipped down and off without any risk of catching. The times when a hawk will do this are when she is alone, either hooded or unhooded, and at these times there should be no danger of her bating and therefore no necessity for tying the tail. When she is taken on to the fist again the tail can be retied, and it is better to take this trouble than to run the risk of a broken feather. After the bath they are of course almost sure to slip it off, while pluming themselves; and indeed it is as well before putting them at the bathing place to cut or draw it off so that all the feathers may be well wetted, and that this may be no obstacle in the way when the bather spreads them out to dry in the sun and air. These directions of course apply to all hawks, which may be much more confidently handled on the fist, especially by inexperienced falconers, when the tails are tied up so as not to break when there is a sudden pressure on them against the hand, as the hawk bates or flinches from the hood. Sparrow-hawks and other small hawks should not be hooded as a rule—at least it is not the modern fashion so to do, though in ancient times there is no very conclusive evidence that they were not kept hooded like the rest. But every hawk, no matter of what species, should be well broken to the hood, and in practice this lesson is better given at the very first as soon as the bird is taken up from hack. The small hawks, unless they are pretty early accustomed to "pull through the hood"—that is to say, to eat their food while wearing the hood—are often only to be induced to do so with much trouble. But the first time that the hood is put on they always make a great to-do, jerking the head in all directions, and snapping at anything which touches them. At such times, therefore, it is easy to put a piece of soft meat in the way of the beak, and if the hood has a large opening (as it should when first put on) some of the meat thus unconsciously pecked at will find its way into the mouth and be swallowed. From the beginning she soon learns to pull through the hood, and the food serves to pacify the angry bird for the infliction she is called upon to endure.

It was the opinion of Sir John Sebright that Sparrow-hawks are, upon the whole, more difficult to manage than larger hawks, and, from his experience as a practical falconer, he was well qualified to give an opinion. They must be kept, he says, in high condition, and cannot fly when there is the least wind. They should be housed also in a dry place, free from draughts. They will take partridges at the beginning of the season, and are the best of all hawks, he says, for landrails.* To show what may be done by careful training, he adds, "I once took a wild partridge with a Sparrow-hawk of my own breaking ten days after it had been taken wild from a wood." †

---

* In Chafin's "History of Cranbourn Chace, 1818, p. 41, reference is made to hawks "annually trained in the neighbourhood of Bridport, Dorsetshire, for taking landrails in the hemp and flax fields near that town, in which in some seasons they are very plentiful."

† "Observations upon Hawking," 1828, p. 52.

TRAINING THE GOSHAWK.

It may be safely asserted that no one gets to know much about falconry until he has contrived, by some blunder or other, to lose a few hawks; and it is equally certain that many a man would like to try his hand at it, did he not believe that the sport is attended with greater difficulty than is really the case. One cause of failure at starting is the selection of a hawk which is quite unsuited to the country in which it is to be flown. A man residing, perhaps, in a woodland district procures a Peregrine Falcon—a long-winged, high-flying hawk. "Rook-hawking" for him is out of the question. The rooks are able to "put in" at once, there is no flight, and no kill. He tries his hand at partridges in September. The hawk "rings up," and in doing so disappears temporarily behind some wood. The owner, missing her, gets alarmed, and runs wildly through, or round, the wood to catch sight of her again. Meanwhile the hawk is mounting, and by this time, perhaps, is once more over the spot from whence she was flown, and is "waiting on" beautifully in expectation of a covey being flushed. This game of "hide and seek" proceeds until the hawk, disappointed, goes away down wind, and is lost—for the time being, at all events. The moral of this is, never fly a falcon in an enclosed country, where you cannot keep her in sight, and where she cannot see the lure if need be. In some measure this will apply to Lark-hawking with Merlins, unless there are some big open fields, with little or no covert down wind into which the quarry may escape, for larks, although good fliers, especially if clean moulted, and able at times to distance the hawk, are very apt, when covert is near, to lose heart and drop into it, seeking safety in concealment rather than in flight.

For a woody, hill and dale country, then, or an enclosed district with big hedgerows, a short-winged hawk is the best; and if there are plenty of rabbits, a Goshawk is the bird to show sport—not only with rabbits and hares (if the hawk be of the more powerful female sex), but also moorhens, landrails, partridges, and even pheasants, if found in the open sufficiently far from covert to give a flight. For a less ambitious falconer, of course, a female Sparrow-hawk will show sport with smaller quarry, and some pretty flights may be had at Blackbirds and Thrushes in the turnip fields.

A good Goshawk should have a small head, large eyes, beak long and black, neck long, breast full, claws large and long, feet and legs of a greenish colour (verds).*

It is generally asserted and believed that the Goshawk is a troublesome bird to train, requiring

* Nicholas Bonnefous, "Traité de Fauconnerie," 1681, p. 52.

FEMALE GOSHAWK ON BOW-PERCH.
From a Photograph by Reginald Lodge.

much carrying to render her docile—to "man" her, as the old falconers would say*—and careful dieting to keep her in condition. This is true of most hawks, but a good deal will often depend upon the temperament of the individual bird. Hawks are as different in their dispositions as human beings, and on this account some will train in half the time that others will require for the purpose.

To show how little real difficulty there is in the matter for any one disposed to try and train a Goshawk, it may be of interest to describe the experience of the writer. In the month of August, a young female Goshawk, sound, and in good feather, was procured in France and despatched to London, where she arrived in a lined hamper (as described on p. 16), hooded, and without any damage to her train or flight feathers. She was taken out of the basket in a darkened room, set upon the perch, unhooded, and left quiet for a time to "rouse" and rest after her long journey. She was then fed, on the glove, of course, and although very shy at first, and "bating off" several times, she gradually gained confidence, and commenced to feed. Under these circumstances a hawk will not be hurried; there is nothing for it but to be very patient, keeping as quiet as possible, and giving the bird time to look about her. If, after a little while, she does not appear to notice the meat which is held in the glove, a gentle squeeze of the foot will

---

* Shakespeare says: "Another way I have to man my haggard, to make her come and know her keeper's call."—"Taming of the Shrew," act iv., sc. i.

cause her to look down and see it, and, after a little examination, she will probably pull at it, and, finding it good, will go on till she has got half a crop.

Leaving her on the perch all night, and unhooded,* the next morning before breakfast began the serious business of carrying the hawk and "manning" her. Always approaching the perch very quietly, and taking her off with a bit of meat, she was carried about the room for some time, then gently hooded, and taken out of doors. The hood was necessary to ensure a safe passage through a crowded thoroughfare, *en route* for a London park. Once on the grass and away from the crowd, the hood was removed, and the bird allowed to look about, and get gradually accustomed to people passing at a distance. If any one ran up suddenly to stare, or a dog appeared upon the scene, the hood was popped on again, till the danger of alarming the bird had passed. For a couple of hours, morning and afternoon, would the bird be carried in this way, getting tamer every day, and requiring less and less hooding. Gradually she was induced to come from the perch to the fist, at first only stepping on to the glove, held close to her, then a few inches off, finally at a little distance; a well-garnished lure being shown her as an inducement.

---

* There is a difference of opinion among falconers whether Goshawks and Sparrow-hawks should ever be hooded. Nicholas Bonnefous, writing in 1681, says: "Celuy qui souffre le chaperon vaut mieux que celuy qui n 'en veut point, car il s'en bat moins." See also the remarks in favour of the hood by Mr. W. H. St. Quintin, quoted on p. 143.

The next lesson was to fling the lure down on the grass and let her go off the fist on to it, repeating this a few times, and varying the performance by making her jump to the fist from the ground. When she did this well, it was time to "enter" her at the quarry she was destined to fly at, and she was now ready to go to the country for that purpose. Arrived there, the last stage of the training commenced with the aid of a friend.

Procuring a freshly killed rabbit, we tied a light line to the two fore-legs, and got a boy to draw it at full speed over the grass at a given signal, the hawk (with a line to her swivel) being allowed to go off the fist as soon as the rabbit began to move, care being taken, of course, to fly her when she was keen, in the afternoon, just before feeding time. She flew with a will at the first attempt, and took the rabbit with a good grip. Walking very slowly and quietly towards her, so as not to alarm her or let her suppose the quarry was about to be taken from her, we just cut a slit or two in the back of the rabbit's neck, and let her have a mouthful or so of the still warm flesh. This by way of encouragement. A second flight, at a greater distance, and the bird was then fed up and carried home, still feeding on the glove as she went.

A more promising hawk could not be found, for she was both good-tempered and courageous—two most desirable attributes in a Goshawk. She had flown so well to the dead lure that we now determined to give her a live rabbit under conditions that would be favourable to her. The ferrets were brought into requisition, and in an hour's time we had secured two nice rabbits for our purpose. A large and heavy flowerpot being inverted on the grass, a capital trap was extemporised with a long line and cross-piece of wood through the aperture. "Jesses" were then put on the rabbit's hind legs, with a coil of "creance," or line, to run out when he bolted, the hawk being then flown loose. Over went the trap, out went the rabbit at his best pace (running out his line like a salmon) and off went the hawk in pursuit. The grass being short, all went well, and the rabbit was cleverly captured and held until it was quickly and mercifully despatched by the falconer.

A repetition of this lesson with another bagged rabbit, and the hawk was pronounced ready to be flown loose at a wild one.

It was an anxious moment as we walked the next afternoon about a rough bramble-covered common, in anticipation of getting a good flight at a rabbit. A couple of beaters tried the most likely looking bushes, while we stood in the open, "with grey Goshawk on hand" (as Chaucer hath it), waiting for a rabbit to bolt.

At length we were rewarded. Out flashed a bunny, and across the open like lightning. Unfortunately, the space to be crossed was too short; and, although the hawk left the hand instantly, the rabbit just contrived to reach a bush before she could seize him; but so plucky was she that she went in after him, and got so far into the bush—through which, of course, he made his escape

—that we had to use our knives and cut her out to prevent damage to feathers. This was bad luck for a beginning, but the hawk was keen, and we could easily find another for her. This we did, and she took him in style—a great big buck rabbit, who

FIG. 24.—GOSHAWK AND RABBIT.
From a drawing by G. E. Lodge.

thought to get rid of her by jumping into the air and kicking like any "buckjumper," but she stuck to him well till we killed him, when she was duly rewarded.

The critical stage was now passed. The hawk had killed wild quarry, and was "made." All she wanted now was practice, and this we took care she should get; for while the mornings were devoted to Partridge shooting, the afternoons were spent in hawking, flying Merlins as well as the Goshawk, and enjoying a fair measure of success. Rabbit after rabbit succumbed upon the common, moorhen after moorhen in the marsh, and as the season wore on, the sport was varied by an occasional flight at a pheasant which, rising in the open at a sufficient distance from any covert, afforded an opportunity not to be missed.

Looking back at the various stages of this bird's training, it does not appear to have been a matter of any difficulty. If any part of the business can be called troublesome, it is the preliminary "carrying" for several hours a day. This, however, is necessary, and should not be deputed. A hawk should know no perch but her owner's fist. She will thus become as attached to him as a dog, jumping on to his glove from her block, showing her contentment to be with him, and manifesting a keen appreciation of the sport which both have learnt to enjoy in delightful companionship.

The following remarks by Captain F. H. Salvin on the management of the Goshawk are so practical and so much to the point as coming from an experienced falconer, that they deserve to be quoted here. Writing in *The Field* of April 13, 1889, he says:—

Until Mr. Birch, of Wretham, some forty years ago, obtained a male Goshawk through the Loo Hawking Club, no hawk of this kind had been used in England since the days of Colonel

Thornton, who left England early in this century, and went to reside in France, where he died in 1823. This information I received from John Tong, who had been in the service of Colonel Thornton as keeper and assistant falconer, and was afterwards one of Lord Harewood's keepers. In 1851, I was introduced in London to the late William Burckhardt Barker, who for many years had resided in an official capacity at Tarsus. In a work which he published on "Cilicia and its Governors," he has given an interesting account (p. 284) of hawking as practised there; but, though his management of the Goshawk was most successful, he evidently knew little about falcons, which, apparently, are not used much in Cilicia. I found him a most enthusiastic admirer of the Goshawk. His system of training was never to hood the bird, except when travelling, and he began its training by carrying it at night by lamp-light, in the streets. My first Goshawk—Juno—was obtained through him, and her first lessons (called "manning") were given in the busiest streets in London. I soon found how quiet a Goshawk remains by lamplight, and that the passing to and fro of men, horses, and dogs, had, after a time, but little effect upon her nerves. In these nocturnal rambles the hawk was encouraged to feed off the hand. In a short time the day training commenced, viz., coming to the hand from a field gate, or rail, for meat held out to her, as described so well by Mr. Harting in *The Field* of January 26, 1889 (*ut supra*, pp. 127-134).

The short-winged hawks (the Sparrow-hawk and Goshawk) are remarkably different from the long-winged falcons, not only in disposition, but also in their feathers and mode of flight. For instance, they can turn in a wonderfully small space, which the long-winged hawks cannot do; they get up their pace at once, and, from the peculiar nature of their feathers, can dash into such thick covert as sometimes to necessitate the bushes being cut away to get them out, when their owl-like plumage will be found not to have suffered in the least. The Goshawk and Sparrow-hawk clutch their prey, and are so quick about it that I have known a Goshawk to catch a rat in each foot when several had been bolted from the same hole by a ferret.

The short-winged hawks require to be in a condition of keenness, called "yarak," before they can be trusted at large, and when by carrying and proper feeding this happy condition has been attained, they must be kept at work, or carried daily, for idleness will necessitate a renewal of a long course of carrying. You may know a hawk is "in yarak" by the wild excited look it assumes, with an elevation of the crest feathers.*

In the wild state the Goshawk feeds twice a day. She often selects an old tree standing outside a forest, within which she finds there is plenty of quarry. At this commanding post she remains for many days, killing what may come out to feed, and coming down again upon what is left in the evening. Compared with a falcon, she is a coarse feeder, slow over her meals, and does not eat so much as the Peregrine.

I always feed my Gos in the evening, giving her half or three-quarters of a crop, and a full crop on Saturdays, the quantity, of course, being regulated by her condition, which may be known by feeling. Anything in the list of quarry killed will do for food for this hawk, but in the case of waterhens and coots it is advisable first to remove the skin and fat, which throws a Goshawk out of "yarak." When she is not earning her own dinner, I give fowls heads, first breaking down the skull and neck bones. I keep her out night and day on the bow-perch, round which is a circle of sand, but put her in the mews in very wet or windy weather.

The form of bow-perch I have devised, and prefer to any other. will be seen in the accompanying illustration, which is a portrait of a Goshawk belonging to me, engraved by Mr. G. E. Lodge from a photograph. The framework of the perch, being of iron, is very strong, comparatively light, and easily moved, being driven into the ground like a croquet hoop, except that, to give greater steadiness, there is a centre leg, broader and twice as long as the two outside ones. The top is lightly padded and covered with saddler's leather to a thickness just sufficient for the hawk to grasp, and a further recommendation is that the hawk, being unable to pass under the hoop, never gets "hung up" by having her leash and jesses twisted. It also prevents diseasd feet. The height of the perch from the ground when the spike is driven down is 10in., and the perch itself about the same; the greatest width below the perch is 16in. Both the Goshawk and Sparrow-hawk should be offered an occasional bath; but, as their long and fluffy under

* The derivation of this word "yarak" we have never been able to discover. We have not found it used in print by any writer antecedent to Captain Salvin, and can only surmise that it may be of Turkish origin, derived from Barker, who does not, however, adopt it in his own work above mentioned.

tail-feathers take long in drying, they are not over fond of the tub.

The variety of quarry that these short-winged hawks will take in a day (for they do not tire like falcons) is extraordinary. Here is a list of the quarry I have taken with a Goshawk: English and Scotch hares, rabbits, pheasants, landrails, wild duck, coots, waterhens, rats, mice, squirrels, stoats, weasels, and once a hedgehog.

FIG. 25.—A MALE GOSHAWK ON THE BOW-PERCH.

In entering at rabbits, a short and light "whippance"* of cane will be found an excellent method of handicapping the quarry, and preventing a rabbit from going to ground. It should be attached

* The "whippance" for carthorses is used to keep the chains apart between wheeler and leader.

by a line to a light collar round the neck; the line, after passing between the legs, is divided, and the two ends tied to the cane at a little distance apart, so as to make it drag.

The jesses should be long, and made of "kip" leather, well greased with a mixture of oil and wax.

Whether the Goshawk should be trained to come "to the fist" or "to the lure" seems at the present day to be a disputed question. According to tradition, and to the teaching of the old masters of falconry, "a hawk should know no perch but her master's fist," and on being flown, should be taught to return to it after an unsuccessful flight.

In a country where trees do not exist, the disappointed Goshawk lights on the ground, as on the moors or open downs. In a wooded district where trees frequently offer a tempting stand for a hawk, which is generally irresistible, it has been found in practice that a swing of the lure (a small dead rabbit on a line answers very well) will bring a Goshawk out of a tree quicker than anything else.

As a staunch Conservative, I am strongly in favour of upholding traditions regarding field sports, if only because they have borne the test of long experience; but, on the other hand, we must make allowance for the altered conditions under which hawking is now practised, and remember that at the present day country gentlemen, with so many more demands upon their time, are unable to give that amount of attention to the training of hawks which our ancestors cheerfully bestowed, and which was, in fact, the secret of their success. Doubtless, if a man can give the time to make his hawk come to the fist, it is more perfect training and more in accordance with the ancient practice; but, as shown in Mr. Harting's article, already quoted, he will get his hawk on much quicker and kill as much with her by making her "to the lure."

Captain F. D. Bland, of Draycott, near Stoke-on-Trent, thus relates his experience with the Goshawk:

A relation of mine having given me permission to hawk rabbits on his estate in Yorkshire, I made a fresh start with two hawks—an untrained eyess female, which I obtained from Mr. Henri Lefebvre, of Paris, and an adult female, which I bought from Sir Ralph Payne-Gallwey. I soon got the former into working order, and killed a lot of rabbits with her, but unfortunately she died during her first moult; and with the old hawk of Sir Ralph's I have had grand sport. Last year, besides a heavy bag of rabbits, I killed two hares with her. I slipped her at six hares altogether, and she flew at each one with great determination, and caught them all, but four of them, after a splendid "rough and tumble," managed to get the best of it, and kicked themselves free before I could get up to her assistance. One was a really magnificent struggle. I let her go at a big hare which jumped up some 40 yards ahead in a large pasture; on her first "binding" to it, hare and hawk went twice head over heels, and then, the hawk slipping her hold, puss went on alone, leaving her on the ground; but she was not yet defeated, for she picked herself up, and again overtook and struck the hare, only to be kicked off again after another struggle. A third time did this plucky Goshawk make off after the hare, which by this time had managed to reach the shelter of a small flock of sheep, and very cleverly ran under them and escaped. The hawk, dead beat, "took stand" in a small fir tree. My companion, a brother officer now serving his country and his Queen in the malarial swamps of West Africa, was delighted, and declared it was one of the most sporting things he had ever witnessed. Of the two hares killed, one was quite dead by the time I reached her.

I have just returned from a two months' visit to the same estate, and the old hawk's bag is seventy rabbits, two stoats, and a rat or two. I did not fly her at hares this season. My best day's bag was four couple of rabbits, bolted by ferrets, in about two hours. I often had to bolt the rabbits, as the country has been generally too wet for them to lie out. I have seen rabbits taken in all sorts of places and positions. I once saw my hawk, in pursuit of a rabbit, fly right down a large hole in the rock in the side of a quarry, and watched her drag the rabbit out of it. This was in the well-known Jackdaw Crag, near Bramham Moor, where Colonel Thornton used to fly his falcons at herons on passage.

I have seldom had much bother with hawks "taking stand" in a tree, and refusing to come down to the lure. A piece of rabbit —a hind leg or head and shoulders—tied to a string and thrown up to her generally brings her down, and is much more attractive than a whole dead rabbit. The best way to use the latter is not to throw it, but, having paunched it, to leave it on the ground some little way off, with the inside well exposed. The really important thing is the management of the food. I always gorge my hawk on a Saturday, letting her eat as much as she will of the best lean beef, and she will fill her crop till she staggers under the weight of its contents. She gets nothing on Sunday, nor, if she is at all dilatory about coming to the lure on Monday, on that day either. She is well mannered enough on Tuesday. The rest of the week she gets a small portion of rabbit with the fur on, and here experience can only guide one as to the quantity. Of course, in the summer time, during the moult, she eats as much as she likes every day. Should, however, my hawk hesitate about coming down, I take care that my attendant carries a live pigeon as a last resource, and the sight of it invariably brings her down at once. Where rabbits are plentiful, I see no reason why a Goshawk should not kill five or or six couple or more in a day, and the conclusion I have come to, after two seasons' experience, is that the difficulties of training Goshawks are greatly exaggerated.

There was a time, before the art of shooting flying came into vogue, when almost every country gentleman in England kept a Goshawk or two, and very high prices were given for well-trained birds. Even in James I.'s time, after "birding-pieces" had been introduced, good Goshawks fetched a good round sum. Edmund Bert, who published "An Approved Treatise of Hawks and Hawking," in 1619, tells us that he had "for a Goshawke and Tarsell a hundred marks, both solde to one man within sixteen months," and for another he was offered forty pounds, and ultimately sold her for thirty—an extraordinary price, when we consider the relative value of money in those days. At that time, doubtless, there were many places in the British Islands where the Goshawk was to be found breeding, where the nests or eyries were jealously watched, and the young were taken as soon as they were ready to fly. This, however, is a thing of the past.

It is very many years since a Goshawk's nest was found in Great Britain; not since Colonel Thornton, a well-known falconer and good all-round sportsman, discovered one in the Forest of Rothiemurcus, and

FIG. 26.—"SHADOW OF DEATH."

A famous Goshawk belonging to the late T. J. Mann, of Hyde Hall, Sawbridgeworth. Drawn from life by G. E. Lodge.

trained one of the young birds.* This was at the end of the last or beginning of the present century,

* See "A Sporting Tour in the North of England and Scotland," 1804, pp. 107, 136, 137, 154, 155.

since which time no similar discovery has been recorded.

At the present day, the Goshawks trained and flown in England (and we know of many), are procured from France or Germany; chiefly from France, where, thanks to the good offices of some of the French falconers—especially M. Pichot, who has done so much to keep alive the old sport in that country—they are looked after, the nests protected, and the young birds secured at the proper time. The price varies with the age and condition of the bird. You may get one through a dealer for a couple of pounds, but it is a chance whether the flight feathers are unbroken, perfect wings being a *sine quâ non* in the case of a hawk that is to be trained and flown. It is better to pay a little more, as in Paris, and secure a good one. Occasionally a Goshawk is taken in a bow-net by one of the Dutch hawk-catchers in North Brabant, and sent to England; but as a rule the birds captured by them are Peregrines, for which, at the present day, there is greater demand.*

To show what success may be attained even in the first season with a young Goshawk, we may refer to the bag made by a French falconer still living, who, with a young female Goshawk (better than a male bird, because larger and stronger) which he trained himself, took 322 rabbits, 3 hares,

---

* In the spring of 1881, near Darmstadt, according to Col. Delmé-Radcliffe, no less than 42 Goshawks were captured. (See *The Field*, March 12, 1881.

and 2 magpies, and the following season 280 rabbits, 2 leverets, 11 partridges, 4 magpies, and 2 squirrels!

A famous female Goshawk named "Shadow of Death," belonging to the late Mr. T. J. Mann, of Hyde Hall, Sawbridgworth, took in one season 120 rabbits, 9 pheasants, 1 hare, 1 partridge, 3 squirrels, and 13 waterhens.

In the season of 1886 a young male Goshawk, trained by Mr. John Riley, of Putley Court, Herefordshire, took 26 partridges, 10 pheasants, 16 rabbits, 5 landrails, 12 waterhens, and a stoat.

Between November, 1892, and April, 1893, a female Norwegian Goshawk, belonging to Major Ernest Anne, of Blenkinsopp Castle, Greenhead, Carlisle, took 220 rabbits, 1 hare, 15 waterhens, 6 pheasants, 1 rook, 1 stoat; total, 244 head.

Sir Henry Boynton, of Burton Agnes, Yorkshire, in a letter to *The Field*, dated April 28, 1894, stated that a female Goshawk in his possession, in the season of 1892-93, took no less than 340 rabbits and 34 various, and, in the following year, 130 rabbits and 50 various.

The same year Mr. W. H. St. Quintin, of Scampston Hall, Rillington, York, had a young male Goshawk, which he brought from Norway, with which he captured 18 rabbits, 85 waterhens, and a brace of partridges. This hawk, as an experiment, was broken to the hood, and often flown "out of the hood" at the quarry, without in any way affecting his readiness to do his best; while his owner found that "as a matter of convenience, it often permitted the hawk to take his place on the cadge, or on the game cart—where, of course, he could not have stood unhooded—instead of being left at home, and, consequently, unflown:" (*The Field*, June 2, 1894.)

After this no tyro need despair, and though, for want of experience, he may not for some time attain to such success as this, he will at all events discover in the sport of hawking with the Goshawk a most fascinating and enjoyable recreation.

An Old Female Goshawk.

From a Drawing by Schlegel.

SNIPE HAWKING.

EVERY one who has read and admired the books written by that good sportsman and naturalist, the late A. E. Knox,* will doubtless remember the account given by him of the pleasure which he derived, when snipe shooting in the West of Ireland, from observing the way in which a pair of wild Merlins chased and killed his wounded snipe. It is to be found in Letter XI. of his "Ornitholigical Rambles," and might be appropriately quoted here were it not reasonable to suppose that the volume in question stands side by side with the same author's "Game Birds and Wild Fowl," and "Autumns on the Spey," on the bookshelves of those to whom these lines are addressed.

In a letter received from Captain Charles Thompson, dated Charminster, September 22nd, 1890, in which he described the sport which he had just then been enjoying with Merlins flown at Larks, he remarked: "On September 2nd I had a long slip with both hawks at a snipe, and, although they

---

* It was the writer's privilege to be well acquainted with this accomplished sportsman, and his sad lot to have to write a memoir of him when he died in September, 1886. See *The Zoologist*, 1886, p. 453.

flew it for a time, they eventually gave it up. But from what I saw of the flight, I am convinced that if properly worked, 'Snipe hawking' with a cast of Merlins would be the grandest flight obtainable with these beautiful little falcons."

To judge of what may be accomplished in this direction, we have only to turn to Colonel Thornton's delightful "Sporting Tour in the North of England and Scotland," 1804,* in which will be found a description of the sport which he enjoyed in hawking snipe with Peregrine falcons and a tiercel. A single extract will suffice (p. 143):

> We killed twenty-two birds (grouse), and had a most incomparable flight at a snipe, one of the best I ever saw, for full sixteen minutes. The falcon flew delightfully, but the snipe got into a small juniper bush near us, her only resource. I ordered the tiercel to be leashed down, and took the other falcon, meaning at any rate that they should succeed with this snipe. When flushing it, I flew my falcon from the hood, the other was in a very good place, and over the falconer's head. A dreadful well maintained flight they had, and many good buckles in the air. At length they brought it like a shot from the clouds into the same juniper bush it had saved itself in before, and close to which we were standing. "Pluto" soon stood it, and so closely that I fortunately took it alive; and throwing out a moor poult to each falcon as a reward, and preventing by this means the two hawks fighting for the Snipe and carrying it away, we fed them up, delighted beyond measure at this noble flight. We minuted them very accurately both times, when they took the air, and the last flight was eleven minutes, during which time, moderately speaking, they could not fly less than nine miles, besides an infinite number of buckles or turns. The falcon being hooded, and the tiercel not quite fed up, it was proposed by the falconer (Crosley), keen

* A new edition of this work, edited by Sir Herbert Maxwell, Bart., M.P., has been recently published by Arnold, Bedford-street.

after blood, that I should give him a flight with the snipe. This we thought ungenerous, after having afforded us so much sport. We marked him so that we might know him again should he ever come into our hands, and gave him his reprieve and turned him off. He flew very stiff indeed, but would soon recover, as he had received only a very slight stroke from one of the falcons. . . . I once saw a falcon of mine, hawking near Thornville with Captain Barlow, at one stroke cut a snipe in two parts, so that they fell separate.

On one occasion only has the writer seen a snipe killed by a trained falcon. On September 24th, 1887, when grouse hawking with Major Fisher on Riddlehamhope Moor, Northumberland, a young falcon named "Princess" had just been hooded off," and we were ranging for grouse when a full snipe rose almost at our feet. The falcon saw it instantly, and being well placed made a splendid cut at it, killing it with the first stoop. To our surprise she did not attempt to carry, which, with so light a quarry, we were afraid she might have done.

FIG. 27.—A WOUNDED SNIPE.

WOODCOCK HAWKING.

THE opportunities which occur for a flight at a woodcock must be very rare. I have never personally witnessed such a flight, though I have seen and shot many woodcocks in places where hawking was impracticable. There are many parts of the country where, at the proper season, woodcocks may be flushed and shot without much trouble, but where to take one with a long-winged hawk would be impossible owing to the nature of the ground and surrounding covert. The only chance for such a flight is when a cock is found (or flushed and marked down) on a hill side, or in the open at a sufficient distance from any wood or planting to admit of a well placed hawk being able to stoop and kill before the quarry can "put in."

In November, 1889, Major Fisher gave an interesting address on "Modern Falconry" to the members of the Cotswold Naturalists' Field Club, which was subsequently printed in their "Proceedings," * and in the course of his remarks described a flight at a woodcock with one of his own

* Vol. X., Part 1, p. 39, 1889-90.

hawks on a moor near Loch-Eil, in Argyllshire, at a place called Fassiefern. As his narrative will illustrate far better than any words of mine the subject matter of this chapter, and as the journal in which it originally appeared is not readily accessible, I cannot do better than quote it here. He says:

I had made a line to beat out a wide bank of bracken, then brown in early autumn. . . . Suddenly up went a fine woodcock. I unhooded and cast "Taillie" after her, and the flight began.* . . . Up and up she went in long zigzags, with precisely the style and action of her smaller relative the common snipe, but mute. The falcon mounted rapidly in her train, though at a considerable disadvantage at first. I saw it was going to be a long affair, got out my glasses, and lay down on the heather. On one side of me was my then falconer, Jamie Barr, one of the well known family of Scotch falconers; on the other side my gillie, Sandy Kennedy, the proud possessor of the best pair of eyes in all Argyll, if not in the West of Scotland. . . . The woodcock, with the falcon below and behind her, did not dare to come down or return—*vestigia nulla retrorsum* was her motto—and soon the pair of dots were high over the sea loch (there a mile wide), the cock's point being evidently Morven, on the other side of the Strait. . . . But finding herself over the water and unable to shake off her pursuer or gain the distant haven of Morven, she had no alternative but to seek the shelter of the bracken on our side, from whence she sprang; so the poor fowl turned tail, and "went for it" in a long slanting descent from an incredible altitude.

As they both neared us, they presented the appearance of two little balls falling out of the sky right towards us, and quite straight, with the difference (fatal to the poor woodcock) that "Taillie," who began below her was now well above. The hawk was evidently unwilling or afraid to stoop over the water, but the moment the cock was over the land, she shot herself forward and straight in air, instead of slanting, half perpendicularly down,

---

* "Taillie," so called from her broken tail, was a Welsh falcon from the Glamorganshire precipices of the "Worm's Head."

like her quarry (both moving with incredible speed) turned over and stooped. . . . It was fatal this time to the woodcock, for leaving a cloud of feathers behind, she tumbled head over heels before us into the very patch of bracken she came from, and meeting there with an old anthill, bounded off it many a yard, and lay still. The hawk soon recovered herself, and dashed on to her well earned quarry. Needless to say I did not disturb her thereon, but served out the whisky, and drank her health all round.

This well told experience will recall to the minds of many the anecdote related by the late A. E. Knox, in his delightfully written volume, "Game Birds and Wildfowl," concerning the falcon lost by Col. Bonham when hawking for woodcocks in Rossmore Park, co. Monaghan (p. 171); and it establishes, moreover, the truth of Knox's statement written forty years previously (*i.e.*, in 1850) that in woodcock hawking there is much danger of losing the falcon, "for as soon as the woodcock has attained a certain altitude, it will—especially if favoured by a fresh breeze—strike off in a direct line, and lead the hawk a distance of many miles."

Nevertheless, Col. Bonham has known as many as fifty woodcocks procured in the same season by one Peregrine, and Col. Thornton once killed forty-nine in one week with his hawks at Kelester, N.B.*

---

* "Sporting Tour in the North of England and Scotland," 1804, p. 32.

HERON HAWKING.

THE reader of these pages, especially if he be a falconer, will scarcely consider this volume complete without some allusion, however brief, to Heron Hawking, to which poetical reference has been made by such classical English writers as Spenser, Massinger, Somervile, and Walter Scott, to say nothing of the beautiful description given by the Spanish poet Calderon. This old world phase of the sport is, alas! extinct. Why? The conditions necessary for its successful practice no longer exist. It is true there are plenty of herons in the country. Some years ago I ascertained, by the collection of statistics from all parts of the British Islands, the existence of more than 200 heronries.* Some of these comprised more than a hundred nests, and as each nest would annually contain four or five eggs, it is evident that a large number of herons would be scattered about the country. Indeed, one has evidence of this whenever a long railway journey takes one across the open marsh lands, or along the coast where these birds may be seen, sometimes five

---

* See *The Zoologist*, 1872, p. 3261, and Yarrell's "British Birds," 4th edition. Vol. iv., p. 164.

or six together. If nothing but the finding of a heron were necessary for the sport of hawking, there would be no difficulty in the matter.

Nothing would be easier than to walk out into the marshes, "with grey goshawk on hand," find a heron in a drain, stalk it, and on its rising fly the hawk and capture it. But this is not heron-hawking in the proper sense of the term. There would be no sport at all in taking the quarry in this way. What is wanted is a heron passing on the wing at a moderate height, so that the hawk, or hawks (formerly both falcons and jerfalcons were used for this sport) on being "hooded off" would have to "ring up" to get above the heron, an advantage which the latter would always endeavour to prevent by rising also, and a fine ringing flight would be the result. But to effect this it is necessary to have good open country in the neighbourhood of a heronry where the falconer may wait with his hawks and watch for a heron going out light (*i.e.*, empty) or returning laden, intercepting the heron, as it were, on its passage and thus ensuring a good flight.* Now the enclosure of waste lands and the increase of plantations has spoiled the country for heron-hawking; and to realise the nature of the sport, as formerly practised, we have to turn to the narratives of those who, more lucky in their generation, were able to witness it, and who have left records of what was

* A Statute of Henry the Seventh's time (19 Hen. VII., cap. 11) imposed penalties for killing herons in any way except by hawking and with the long bow, and for taking young herons out of the nest.

once possible to English falconers but is so no longer. Early in the century Didlington was said to be the only place in the kingdom where heron-hawking was practised.

The *Norfolk Chronicle* of June 12th, 1823, recorded that "the ancient pastime of Heron hawking is still carried on in this county. The casts of hawks, with four falconers, natives of

FIG. 28.—A HERON IN FLIGHT.

From an engraving by G. E. Lodge.

Holland (to which country they repair annually to catch hawks for the ensuing season), are kept at Didlington Hall, the seat of Major Wilson (afterwards Lord Berners), near to which place there is an extensive heronry." Each afternoon during May and June the sport was carried on by ladies and gentlemen living in the neighbourhood, with many visitors from distant counties, so that frequently a company of 150 was seen in the field. The season of 1822 was very favourable to the sport, and no fewer than 173 herons were taken; but in 1823 the falconers were less fortunate, for, although the flights were longer, and the hawks superior both in breed and training, the herons, owing to the severity of the winter, were more scarce. The spirited description of a flight which took place in Mundford Field during the latter season is worthy of a place in local sporting literature. "The heron," says the narrator, "on its way from the heronry to the fens was seen at a considerable distance going down the wind. He was so far off that the falconers hesitated whether they would venture to unhood their hawks, but one of them having luckily upon his wrist a famous hawk, in whom he had great confidence, cast him off alone. It made instantly at the heron, who mounted higher in the air, though still advancing rapidly in his course. The whole field was instantly in motion, and those persons only who have hunted with some of our crack packs of foxhounds can form an idea of the ardour with which each person, including the ladies, strove to be foremost. The hawk made numberless stoops at the heron, which his activity and stoutness enabled him to avoid, and it was not till some time after the birds had ceased to be visible to the chief part of the field that the hawk was able, after repeatedly striking his quarry, to bring him to the ground. The flight was so rapid that of the numerous party who started with the hawk not more than four or five persons were brought up at this interesting moment. The flight lasted at least twenty-six minutes, and the distance from point to point exceeded six miles. The height to which the birds rose was so great, that, to use the expression of the falconers, 'they were six steeples in the air—no bigger than humble bees.'" It was the custom at Didlington, when a heron was taken alive, to place upon one of his legs a metal ring, upon which was engraved the date and place of his capture. The bird was then turned off to provide sport at some future date. Several of the Didlington herons were afterwards recaptured in Holland, and the *Chronicle* of March 14th, 1835, quoting from a Bristol paper, stated that a heron had been shot near Carmarthen, with a ring around its leg bearing the inscription, "Major Wilson, Didlington Hall, Norfolk, 1822."

The last English falconer who kept Heron hawks was the late Edward Clough Newcome, of Hockwold

Heron Hawking.

From a Painting by G. E. Lodge.

and Feltwell Hall, in the County of Norfolk, who died in September, 1871, and an interesting account, communicated by himself, of two remarkable birds which he possessed, named "Sultan" and "De Ruyter," will be found in Freeman and Salvin's "Falconry: Its Claims, History, and Practice," 1859. These hawks were brought from Holland by the Dutch falconer, Jan Pells, and in one year took 54 herons, and in the following season 57 herons. For further details the reader may be referred to the memoir of their owner in my Bibliography of Falconry* (p. 257), where also will be found details concerning heron-hawking as practised by the Loo Hawking Club, and by that enthusiastic falconer, Colonel Thornton, of Thornville Royal.

Before dismissing the subject of heron-hawking, it may not be amiss to devote a few lines to the contradiction of a popular delusion which has been sanctioned by no less an authority than Sir Walter Scott,† and has been repeated many times in print. It is to the effect that a heron when hard pressed and stooped at by the falcon will point his beak upward and receive the descending hawk upon its sharp extremity, thereby disabling, if not killing it outright. There is not only no authority for this very pretty story, but we have the direct testimony of eye-witnesses that it has never happened within their experience. When the members of the Loo Hawking Club used to meet annually for heron-

* *Bibliotheca Accipitraria*, published by Quaritch in 1891.

† See his description, in "The Betrothed," chap. xxiii., of a flight at a heron with two falcons from the Isle of Man,

hawking in Holland, their hawks used to capture from 150 to 220 herons in a season, and in October, 1877, I was verbally assured by the head falconer to that club, the late Adrian Mollen, that in the hundreds of flights at the heron of which he had been a spectator, he never once witnessed such a manœuvre as that above mentioned. This also was the verdict of the late Edward Clough Newcome, with whose hawks many a heron was taken in the wilds of Norfolk.

FIG. 29.—A DEAD HERON. By Mme. Muraton.

KITE HAWKING.

To see kite-hawking at the present day one must visit India, where the Saker (a hawk practically unknown in England) is trained for the purpose, and flown by native princes as well as by a few enthusiastic English falconers whose military duties detain them in districts suited to the pastime.

But there was a time when kite-hawking was the sport of princes in this country—when king and court rode out of London to the great heaths of Royston, Newmarket, and Thetford, there to spend several days, or it might be weeks together, in witnessing the splendid flights of trained Jerfalcons belonging to rival falconers.

Whatever may be thought of the follies and foibles of King James I.—and what monarch has been free from them ?—English sportsmen should never forget the encouragement he gave to field sports—and more especially to the sports of hunting, coursing, and hawking—not only by the personal share which he took in them at every opportunity, and the sums of money he lavished in the purchase of horses, hounds, and hawks, with all that was necessary to maintain them, but also by the pains he took to entertain at court the leading sportsmen of foreign countries whose knowledge and skill displayed in friendly rivalry went far to revive traditions of sport that might otherwise have been lost.*

In 1624 a French falconer had arrived in London with a present of hawks, horses, and setting dogs from Louis XIII., and the king, against the advice of his physicians, went to Newmarket to see some of the hawks flown. Chamberlain, writing to Sir Dudley Carleton on Jan. 17, from London, says: "He made a splendid entry with his train by torchlight, and will stay till he has instructed some of our people in this kind of falconry, though he costs his majesty £25 to £30 a day." The Exchequer accounts show the following payments:

Expensis of the diet of Mons. Bonavons, a falconer at Royston and Newmarket, in the months of January and February, viz., at Waltham Cross, £34 17s. 8d.; Royston, £41 7s. 7d.; Newmarket (where a prolonged stay was made), £215 11s. 6d.· Then on the return journey, Royston, £43 10s. 2d.; Waltham Cross, £49 8s. 9d.; and London, £354 11s. 9d.; thirty-five days in the said months, amounting altogether to the sum of £739 7s. 4d.

It is to be regretted that no record has been found of the nature of the instruction imparted by this French falconer in return for all this outlay.

Sir Thomas Monson was then the King's "master falconer," and in truth, says Sir Anthony Weldon (in a scarce little book entitled "The Court and Character of King James," 1650),

such an one as no prince in Christendom had; for what flights other princes had, he would excel them for his master, in which one was at the Kite.

* See La Curne de St. Palaye, "Mémoires sur l'ancienne Chevalerie," ed. Nodier, tom. ii. p. 378.

The French king (he continues) sending over his faulconers to show that sport, his master faulconer lay long here, but could not kill one Kite (ours being more magnanimous than the French Kite). Sir Thomas Monson desired to have that flight in all exquisitenesse, and to that end was at £1000 charge in Jerfaulcons for that flight; in all that charge he never had but one cast [*i.e.*,

FIG. 30.—A JERFALCON. After Schlegel.
(Formerly flown at the Heron and Kite.)

two falcons] would perform it: and these had killed nine Kites, which were as many as they were put off unto, not any one of them escaping.

To this narrative of Sir Anthony Weldon is to be

traced back the erroneous statement printed in the earlier editions of Yarrell's "British Birds," and repeatedly copied by other authors, to the effect that such high prices were paid for hawks in the reign of James I., that Sir Thomas Monson gave £1000 for a cast—that is, for two; whereas, as above shown, the truth was that he spent £1000 before he succeeded in securing two Jerfalcons which he considered perfect for kite-hawking—a very different story, and one quite likely to be true, seeing that men had to be sent to Denmark, Norway, or Iceland, to capture the falcons in the first place, and the cost of the voyage and maintenance of the men during their absence had to be provided for.

Whereupon (continues Sir Anthony Weldon) the Earle of Pembroke, with all the lords, desired the king but to walk out of Royston towne's end to see that flight, which was one of the most stateliest flights in the world, for the high mountee. The king went willingly forth, the flight was showed, but the Kite went to such a mountee, and the Hawke after her, as all the field lost sight of the Kite and Hawke and all, and neither Kite nor Hawke were either seen or heard of to this present, which made all the court conjecture it a very ill omen.

A curious sequel to this story, not given by Sir Anthony Weldon, and too long to be quoted here, will be found in the third volume of the "Transactions of the Norfolk and Norwich Naturalists' Society" (p. 87), in an article by the present writer on "Hawking in Norfolk."

Kite-hawking, as above remarked, was considered by connoisseurs to be the stateliest of all flights, and it may well be asked, what was there in the

THE FORK-TAILED KITE OR GLEAD.
From a Drawing by Schlegel.

sport to render it so attractive? In the first place, it should be observed that in fine weather it is the natural habit of the kite to soar at a considerable height in the air, either on the look out for prey below, or in the enjoyment of its freedom, and on this account it was (with the exception of the heron) the very best quarry for high-flying hawks. In the next place, its splendid power of wing, enabling it to mount well, and to avoid with comparative ease (until too hardly pressed) the stoops of a trained falcon, caused a flight to be longer sustained and carried on at a greater height than was possible with any other quarry, the heron alone excepted. On this account kite-hawking was considered the very perfection of falconry, and but for the expense attending it would have been still more popular. At the present day, of course, the extinction of the kite in England, and the great difficulty of obtaining Jerfalcons, has practically put an end to this fascinating branch of the sport.

So far as can be ascertained from the scattered annals of hawking in England, the Saker falcon was never much used in this country, though occasional mention of the prices paid for Sakers is to be found in some of the old "Household Books," notably in the "Privy Purse Expenses" of Henry VIII., in whose reign kites were protected by law on account of their utility as scavengers. Apparently the French falconers had better opportunities of procuring the Saker. Woolley, in his "Present State of France," 1687, observes: "The flight at the kite was performed with Jerfalcons, Tiercelets, or Tassels (*i.e.*

the male of the Jerfalcon), and sometimes Sakers; and there was always a decoy to draw the kite to a reasonable height to give him to the hawks."

This was a very curious part of the performance, and deserves special notice.

The kite, as has been said, was espied soaring at a considerable height, often at too great a distance to be flown at with any chance of success; for at sight of the hawk it would at once commence soaring still higher, and, by keeping above its pursuer, would contrive to avoid the fatal stoop. Before any sport could be shown, therefore, it was necessary, by some artifice, to bring down the kite to a reasonable height from the ground. To effect this they resorted to the following curious device: A tame Eagle-owl (called by the French falconers *Le grand duc* and by the Germans *Uhu*) was liberated with a fox's brush tied to its jesses. Flapping slowly along in the glare of day, with this appendage dangling below it, the observant kite was deceived into the belief that it was carrying prey, and, after the manner of its kind, at once descended to play the part of robber. As soon as it had come within a reasonable distance of the hawking party, a Jerfalcon was unhooded and cast off, and the real sport commenced.

There are two illustrations of this sport in a series of folio engravings by Ridinger, published about 1760, in which the Eagle-owl conspicuusly figures.

No one has left a better description of the incidents of kite-hawking than the French falconer Charles D'Arcussia, whose treatise on Falconry, founded on personal experience, is one of the best that has been written. It deserves to be better known, for it contains not only much practical advice on training and managing hawks of all kinds, but also the most graphic descriptions of the flights which the author witnessed when accompanying his master, Louis XIII., on his hawking excursions. But, alas! this book has now become so scarce as to be practically unprocurable. In his forty-sixth letter D'Arcussia treats of the *haute volerie,* as this branch of the sport was termed, and explains how a falcon was trained to kill kites. One of the latter birds having been trapped, or snared, alive, its eyes were "seeled" (that is, closed, by having a silken thread passed through the eyelids and tied—an almost painless operation), and it was set at liberty with a chicken of its own colour tied to its feet. The falcon, which was in readiness to be "entered," and, of course, fasting, was then flown at it, and on bringing it down was allowed to feed on the chicken, while the kite's life was spared. After several of such preparatory lessons, the falcon was flown at a wild kite, and rewarded with a brown chicken adroitly substituted for the real quarry.

In his "Conference des Fauconniers" (the second day), D'Arcussia gives an account of a day's kite-hawking, which is too long to be quoted here in its entirety, but which may be briefly and freely translated as follows:

The sport commences by flying an Eagle-owl trailing a fox's brush, this being the first step taken to bring the kite within a reasonable distance. As soon as that is accomplished, they cast off a male Saker, or a Jer-tiercel, then two Sakers, and often a Jerfalcon for a fourth, or four Jerfalcons altogether. From the behaviour of these birds, at first sight it might be supposed that they had no designs upon the kite; but they merely shape their flight to gain the ascendancy, taking advantage of the wind. One day (he continues) I saw four Jerfalcons thus flown. On leaving the fist each took his own course. The kite was not long in perceiving their designs, and did all he could to keep above them. In spite of his efforts, however, they gradually reached the same altitude, and little by little got above him. Then ensued a fine sight. A Jerfalcon named Ostarde was the first to begin, and made his first stoop from a height of more than 20 fathoms (120ft.). The others then stooped in turn; not all at once, but one after another, like hammers on an anvil, making a grand sound with the whizzing of their wings. At it they went, ding-dong, first one and then another, the Kite doing all he could to escape the stoops, turning first to one side then to the other, even turning over so as to show his claws, as if that would deter his assailants, but all to no purpose. The ardour of his pursuers increased as his own courage waned. Not knowing which way to turn, he commenced to scream, and at that moment one of the Jerfalcons seized him, the others "bound" to him, and all five birds came down together. The falconers ran up, the king well to the front, and the Sieur de Luyne, who had charge of this flight, getting hold of the kite as quickly as possible to prevent it from injuring any of the hawks, the latter were taken up one by one, and fed upon a chicken resembling the kite in colour, the flesh of the latter being rank and bad for them.

After describing another flight, D'Arcussia adds that the king was so good natured that he would often spare the lives of the kites, and taking them back with him to Paris, would, after marking them, let them fly out of the windows of the Louvre.

From the sport which this bird provided for royalty, it came to be known as the Royal Kite, *Milan royal* of the French falconers, and *Milvus regalis* of scientific authors. Sanctioned as it is by long usage, it would be well that this name should be retained.

The last kite-hawking seen in England was probably with the Jerfalcons belonging to Lord Orford and Col. Thornton in 1773, and those of Mr. Colquhoun, of Wretham, near Thetford, in 1785. Brandon Warren, Eriswell, and Elden Gap, in Suffolk, Thetford Warren and Croxton Heath, in Norfolk, and Alconbury Hill, in Huntingdonshire, on account of the number of kites to be found there, were favourite localities for the sport.

Some evidence of the former abundance of kites about Alconbury Hill is furnished by Mr. Birch Reynardson in his book on "Stage Coaches." He writes:

> Within a few miles of Stilton, and between Stilton and Stamford, is a hill called Alconbury Hill. In the days I am writing of—about the year 1824, and from before that time to 1828 or 1829—there used to be in that part of the country an incredible number of kites—the forked-tail kite — or what in Scotland were called "gleads," the red feathers of whose forked tail were famous for wings of salmon flies. These birds used to be soaring over the road, and over a wood called Monk's Wood. In almost every direction one used actually to see them sitting in the middle of the road; and on one occasion I remember counting as many as twenty-seven in the air at the same time. The preservation of game, I suppose, has got rid of them, for no such bird is to be seen now (1875), and it is wonderful how in a few years these birds have become almost extinct throughout England. I have not seen one for at least thirty years.*

Prof. Newton has remarked in the fourth edition of Yarrell's "British Birds" (p. 95) that when the

---

*Birch Reynardson, "Down the Road; or, Reminiscences of a Gentleman Coachman," 1875, p. 74.

first edition of that work was published, the woods near Alconbury Hill were still the breeding places of the kite, but it was extirpated there about the year 1844, or soon after. One of the last specimens procured there was forwarded in the flesh to Henry Doubleday, of Epping, by whom it was skinned and very well preserved. At his death it passed into the possession of the late Richard Ashby, of Egham, at the sale of whose collection it was purchased by the present writer as a curious relic of the past.

One of the finest bird pictures ever painted by Joseph Wolf depicts a kite seized by two Jerfalcons as in the last act of the drama described by the French falconer. This original oil painting, in the possession of Lord Lilford, was exhibited in the Grosvenor Gallery at the Sports and Arts Exhibition in the spring of 1890, and was reproduced in the *Field* of 10th January, 1891. For the use of a smaller block, which appeared in the *Magazine of Art* for March, 1896, in illustration of an article by me on "Sport in Art," I am indebted to the courtesy of the editor of that Journal.*

---

* In an article on the disappearance of the kite which I contributed to the *Field* of Dec. 11, 1897, will be found many additional details concerning the former haunts of this bird in England.

KITE-HAWKING WITH GERFALCONS.

From an Oil Painting by Joseph Wolf, in the possession of Lord Lilford.

TRAINED EAGLES.

THE courage and perseverance with which Eagles will pursue hares and rabbits, and even attack prey much larger and heavier than themselves, has no doubt suggested the experiments which have from time to time been made by falconers to train them for the chase. That the Golden Eagle in a wild state will attack not only roe deer, but even red deer, has been placed beyond doubt by the testimony of eye-witnesses.

Capt. Thos. Fraser, of the Argyll and Sutherland Highlanders, writing in the *Field* of March 31, 1888, narrates the following curious occurrence as "not unprecedented in the Highlands:"

On March 22, as my father's Stroneldirg keeper, John Ross, was walking over his ground, accompanied by Lord Lovat's keeper of the neighbouring moor—Killin—they saw five red deer leave a small piece of birch wood, and stand looking about them for a little. Three Golden Eagles appeared, and very shortly attacked one of them—a hind. She immediately bolted at full speed, followed by the eagles, and, after going about three hundred yards, one of the eagles drew himself together, hovered, pounced, and fixed on her head, holding on for about five of her strides, when she fell head over heels, and thus ridded herself of the first eagle for the time. This occurred about a dozen times, the eagles coming to the attack in turns over ground hard with frost. In about ten minutes the hind seemed exhausted, and then the keepers were able to get up to her, finding that the poor beast was quite stupefied, her left hind leg broken, her tongue hanging six inches out, and her mouth open. After smoking a pipe over it, they decided between them that it would be a pity to kill her, as her leg would shortly mend, so they drove her slowly before them into a birch wood, where the eagles, which were still hovering over them, could not well attack her again, and there they left her. She was in good condition, unwounded, and, as John Ross tersely put it, "in good heart."

It must have been a most interesting sight.*

The art of training Eagles, and flying them at hares, foxes, wolves, and small deer, originated in the East, and was introduced into Europe by the Crusaders. The exercise of this art is mentioned by many early writers—as, for example, by Mathew Paris, who died in 1259; by the unknown author of the "Menagier de Paris," which was composed about 1393; and by Crescentius, whose Latin work was printed at Augsburg in 1471, and was followed by a French translation, published in Paris in 1486. Perhaps the earliest writer to deal with the subject from a falconer's point of view was Guillaume Tardif, of Puy en Vellay, a professor at the Collège de Navarre, and reader to Charles VIII. of France (1483—1498), who was a great falconer. His "Livre de l'Art de Faulconnerie," translated, with additions, from the Latin of the Roi Dancus and the Emperor Frederick II., and printed in Paris in 1492, commences with the information that there are three sorts of raptorial birds used for hawking—namely, the Eagle, Falcon, and Goshawk. He refers to different species of Eagle, indicating an

* In Grimble's "Deer Forests of Scotland" (1896) is a capital picture by Thorburn of an Eagle attacking a red deer calf.

Oriental source of information, by giving the Arabic and Syrian names for them, and states that the best are white on the head and back, by which we may presume that he intends the Imperial Eagle (*Aquila imperialis*). The quarry, he says, consists of hare, fox, and gazelle; and a smaller Eagle (perhaps the Steppe Eagle) will take cranes, and other birds. He adds the curious remark that a wild Eagle will chase a trained Goshawk on seeing its jesses, *which it mistakes for prey*, and that the only way to avoid its attacks is to take the jesses off the Goshawk when flying anywhere near the Eagle's haunts.

The Latin work of the Emperor Frederick II., from which Tardif drew much of his information, was in its turn derived to some extent from still earlier treatises in Persian and Arabic, which were translated by the Emperor's physician and secretary. Hence, so far as trained Eagles are concerned, it is not difficult to trace the indebtedness of these authors and their copyists (as Belon, 1555; Bouchet, 1567; and De Thou, 1582) to Oriental sources of inspiration.

In the thirteenth century the Khan of Tartary kept a large number of hawks and Eagles, some of which were trained to catch wolves, and we find confirmation of such feats in the travels of Marco Polo, Leo Africanus, and Pallas. Sir Anthony Shirley relates, in his "Travels," how the Muscovite Emperors used to reclaim Eagles to let fly at hinds, foxes, &c., and adds that one of these was sent as a present to Queen Elizabeth.

Sir John Malcolm, in his "Sketches of Persia,"

and Johnson, in his "Indian Field Sports," both testify to the use of Eagles by Indian and Persian falconers; and Atkinson, in his "Oriental and Western Siberia," describes (pp. 492-494) the way in which a large Eagle, called *Bearcoot*,* is flown at deer and antelope in Chinese Tartary, being carried hooded on a perch which is secured into a socket on the saddle. He says, "No dogs are taken out when hunting with the Eagle; they would be destroyed to a certainty; indeed, the Kirghiz assert that this bird will attack and kill the wolf."

A traveller to the Putrid Sea in 1819 wrote: "Wolves are very common on these steppes, and are so bold that they sometimes attack travellers. We passed by a large one lying on the ground, with an Eagle, which had probably attacked him, by his side. Its talons were nearly buried in his back; in the struggle both had died." ("Memoirs of Stephen Grellet," i., p. 459).

Latham, who refers to the Golden Eagle as being common in parts of Russia, states that at Orenburg these birds are annually exposed for sale, and good ones "sell dear, being used for falconry, to take wolves, foxes, and antelopes." He adds they are used by the Kirghiz (from whom probably the Russians procure them), and often a horse is given for one, when a sheep will purchase another species (Gen. Hist. Birds, 1821, vol. i., p. 56). Many of the writers above quoted refer in terms of admiration

---

* *Barkut* or *Berkut* of the Russians, *Bjurkut* of the Tartars. It is curious that the Welsh name applied both to the kite and buzzard is *Barcud*. How is this similarity to be explained?

to the prowess of a trained Eagle, and remark that if it were not for their great weight, their power of long fasting, and the trouble of training them unless taken quite young, they would certainly be oftener seen in the possession of European falconers. It was doubtless on account of these drawbacks that even such enthusiastic falconers as some of the French Kings were (Henri IV. and Louis XIII. for example) drew the line at Eagles. Charles d'Arcussia, who has left us such graphic descriptions of the hawking exploits of these two kings, relates that a gentleman of Provence took the trouble to procure and tame an Eagle which he offered as a present to Henri IV., but was only laughed at for his pains. In England, so far as I have yet discovered, very little concerning trained Eagles has been placed on record.

Matthew Paris tells us in his "Chronicle" that a young man in the service of the Bishop of London had a Sea Eagle which he had trained to take teal; but, as he goes on to say that this bird would leave its feathered quarry to drop upon a fish, we may infer that it was probably an Osprey. The Osprey's diet is not confined exclusively to fish. Colonel Montagu states that one of these birds was seen to stoop and carry off a young wild duck, half grown, from the surface of the water at Slapton Ley. That the Osprey was formerly trained to take fish may be inferred from the fact that an Act passed in the reign of William and Mary prohibited at a certain season of the year the taking of salmon of any age *by hawks*, racks, gins, &c. Ospreys were certainly kept by James I., and maintained with cormorants and otters on the Thames at Westminster, where, in 1618, the King had special buildings erected for their accommodation, as I have elsewhere fully described ("Essays on Sport," p. 429). But whether these Ospreys were used like the cormorants for taking fish, or were flown, like hawks, at teal, duck, moorhens, and other waterfowl, there is no evidence to show. The chief objection to the employment of the Osprey by falconers would be its habit of carrying its prey to a distance before feeding on it.

Some fifty years ago a Captain Green, of Buckden, in Huntingdonshire, had a tame Golden Eagle, which he had trained to catch hares and rabbits, and which was taken to the field on a perch carried horizontally by two men. It was said to be fairly tractable, but its great weight, and the difficulty of keeping it keen (or "in yarak," as some falconers term it*), owing to its power of fasting, made it too troublesome to manage satisfactorily.

Tame Golden Eagles in outdoor aviaries may be said to be common enough. I have seen several that would take food (generally a dead rat or part of a rabbit) from the hand when called; but this was always done with a mistrustful snatch, made with such force that few persons would care to experience it. The late Mr. Pike, of Achill Island, co. Mayo, had a Golden Eagle in an aviary, the roof of which, being of iron rails, was open to the sky;

---

* See p. 136, note.

THE OSPREY.

Formerly kept by James the First on the Thames at Westminster.

and he affirmed that at the approach of the nesting season, when his bird got restless and noisy, its cries would attract the attention of a wild Eagle, which would come down and for a short time alight close by.

But in none of these cases did the owners put jesses on their birds' legs and attempt to carry and train them. One of the latest instances of a trained Golden Eagle in Western Europe which has come to my knowledge is that of a bird which a few years since was brought from Turkestan by M. Benoit Maichin. I think it must have been in 1883 when, meeting that gentleman in London, I received from him an interesting description of how he acquired it. He had gone with a friend to Turkestan with the object of purchasing some horses of the country, and had had an opportunity of seeing some Kirghis falconers flying their Eagles at hares and foxes. Having never previously seen hawking of any description, he was so fascinated with the sport, that he longed to take home an Eagle with him, with which to astonish his friends in France. For a long time he was unable to prevail upon any Kirghis owner to part with one. The birds had been taken young, at some risk to life or limb, had been trained with great care and trouble, and were valued accordingly. After some persuasion, however, a certain Kirghis, who had set his heart upon a new gun, agreed to give his Eagle in exchange for a gun and £40, and at this high price the bird changed hands. As M. Maichin confessed, he knew nothing about falconry, and as he had no idea how to manage his new acquisition, he engaged a Kirghis servant to look after it, and this man accompanied him on his return to France. It may be readily imagined what a sensation was caused amongst *les amateurs de sport* when this fine bird was flown in their presence. It would come to the lure from a distance of 200 yards if set down on a hillside, or on any elevated spot from which it could easily take wing, and, after several heavy flaps, it would come gliding along straight for the lure, which (if held in the fist with outstretched arm) it would clutch with a shock that made the falconer stagger.

Not having then seen the bird, and being anxious to ascertain its species, I prevailed on the owner to accompany me to the Bird Gallery at the Natural History Museum, with a view to his pointing out a specimen like his own. Pausing before a table case, in which was a Golden Eagle with extended wings, he exclaimed *Voilà mon aigle; mais pas si grand que le mien.* Of this he seemed to have no doubt whatever, though, from his description, I had formed the opinion that his bird was a young Imperial Eagle, or perhaps the Steppe Eagle (*Aquila nipalensis*, Hodgson).

Soon afterwards the novelty of the possession wore off, the owner got tired of his purchase, the Kirghis servant—anxious to return to his own people—was sent back to his native steppes, and the eagle changed hands. It became the property of a well-known French falconer, M. Paul Gervais, of Rosoy, par Acy-en-Multein (Oise), from whom not long afterwards I had an opportunity of hearing how it was managed and flown. M. Gervais gave me a full, true, and particular account, which ran somewhat as follows: As soon as the Eagle, after a judicious course of feeding and fasting, had been got into condition, or "yarak," men were sent out to find a fox, and mark him, if possible, into some spinney, from which he might be easily driven. Beaters were then posted in such a way as to force him to take across the open. As soon as he was viewed away, the Eagle was slipped, and, after a few heavy flaps, glided off in swift pursuit, soon overtaking, with apparent ease, the retreating fox. His tactics were noteworthy. As soon as he came near enough to attack the quarry, he struck him with one foot only, which was generally planted on the loins; the other foot being held in reserve, or, as it were, "on guard." The wisdom of this proceeding was soon evident. The fox thus hard hit turned savagely on the bird, and, making a vicious snap at him, was met full in the face with the Eagle's other foot. The strong and curved claws speedily muzzled him, and, after a few desperate bounds in the air, he almost gave up struggling, being held as in a trap until the falconer ran up, and, with his *couteau de chasse*, gave him the finishing stroke. To a bird that could thus hold a fox, hares and rabbits fell an easy prey, and many a one succumbed to this new and unexpected foe. But at length the day of respite came; the Eagle died, and his owner for the future had to kill his ground game with the smaller but more active Goshawk.

One summer, being in Paris, I had the pleasure of meeting another French falconer, M. Edmond

Barrachin, of Beauchamp, pres Harblay, of whose enthusiasm for hawking I had often heard, and it was with no small satisfaction that I accepted his invitation to pay him a visit, and, Goshawk on hand, go over some of the ground rendered classic by D'Arcussia's descriptions of the flights which he witnessed in the company of Louis XIII. But a stronger incentive was to see his two Eagles, of which I had also heard, one of which was trained to take rabbits. These I found were much smaller than M. Benoit Maichin's bird, and belonged to the species known as Bonelli's Eagle. He had obtained them through a dealer, and had trained one of them in the same way in which a Goshawk is trained.

As we emerged upon the lawn at the back of the house, a pretty sight met our gaze. Seated on their blocks, in various attitudes, were fourteen Goshawks, six Falcons, and the two Eagles aforesaid. On my expressing surprise at his keeping so many, knowing how difficult it would be to find work for them all, he explained that many of them, as I had suspected, were not in flying order, and that, in fact, they were only there because they had been taken from their eyries and offered to him, and he was anxious to save their lives. Fortunately for the object I had in view, one of the Eagles was in flying order, and so was the best Goshawk. With these we took the field. We were favoured with the company of our friend M. Pierre A. Pichot, an original member of the Champagne Hawking Club, and one who has done much of late years to uphold the practice of the old sport in France.

Trained Bonelli's Eagle.

Belonging to M. Edmond Barrachin.

To listen to the jargon of the falconers' art, and share in the animated conversation which ensued as we passed through the woods, carried one back in spirit to the good old days of falconry in France, and, but for our modern costumes, we might have been hawking with Arcussia in the Crau d'Arles, or flying the Goshawk with Boissoudan in the wilds of Poitou.

The day was hot, and there were few rabbits above ground. As we pushed on towards their favourite haunts, we disturbed a number of Indian hog-deer, which, jumping up in front of us, scampered away through the underwood, and disappeared in the distance.

Soon we came to a spot where signs of rabbits were unmistakable, and, choosing a likely hole, a ferret, which we had brought with us, was introduced, while we stood back, holding the Eagle in readiness for a flight. We had not long to wait. A rabbit bolted at a good pace, and the bird was at once slipped. The rabbit, however, was a cunning one, and, instead of bolting straight away (in which case he would have been infallibly overtaken), he suddenly turned sharp to one side and doubled back. The Eagle not being nearly so quick at turning as a hawk, lost ground by this manœuvre, missed the rabbit, and the latter got away. Whereupon the Eagle, after a short flight, took stand upon a neighbouring oak, and had to be brought down to the lure.

The next flight was more successful. Another rabbit was found, and this time essayed to cross an open space between two woods, but the distance was too great, and his speed was unavailing, for the eagle, after a few short flaps, glided off in pursuit, and soon overtook and strangled its prey. It was a novel and interesting sight, though, as an exhibition of falconry, not to be compared with the flight of a falcon at grouse or partridges. Neither did it afford such a spectacle as magpie hawking with a cast of Tiercels, or a mounting lark above a cast of Merlins. But it was a new and never-to-be-forgotten experience, instructive in many ways, and illustrating more forcibly than anything I had seen, man's complete dominion over the fowls of the air.

It would be beside my present purpose to describe the flights at rabbits with the Goshawk which we subsequently enjoyed, and in which the Goshawk showed itself immeasurably superior to the Eagle. Suffice it to say that on reaching home, at my express desire, we weighed the two birds, when the Goshawk turned the scale at 2lb., the Eagle at 4lb. A portrait of the latter bird, engraved by Mr. G. E. Lodge from an excellent photograph, represents it as we saw it sitting upon its block in its French home, under the circumstances above described. In our second illustration, from an instantaneous photograph, it is depicted in the act of killing a rabbit, as here described.

The German name of this bird, *Habichts Adler*, is a good one, as indicating its Goshawk-like appearance and habits. Like the Goshawk, it has a long barred tail, hence the French name for it—*Aigle à queue barée*—and, unlike other Eagles with which we are more familiar, it changes from a dark

Bonelli's Eagle and Rabbit.

From a Photograph by M. Edmond Barrachin.

immature plumage to a lighter adult one, instead of the converse. The Spanish name for it, *Aguila blanca*, applies only to the fully adult male, which is white underneath, with longitudinal streaks of dark brown.

It inhabits Southern Europe, Northern and Central Africa, and ranges eastward into India, but not to China. In the south of Spain it is the commonest rock-breeding Eagle to be found in that country, and a pair is stated to nest annually on the rock of Gibraltar.

In France it is of rare occurrence, and in Germany it has only been met with in the south (in Bohemia), but in parts of Italy and Greece it is not uncommon, and is resident in Sardinia and Sicily. Canon Tristram, who met with it in Palestine, considered it to be more truly a game-killing raptor than any other eagle, and less addicted to carrion feeding. Mr. A. O. Hume writes of it in India as frequenting every large lake in Sindh, making terrible havoc amongst the smaller water birds, and carrying off wounded fowl before one's eyes with the greatest impudence.

These active habits, combined with its moderate size and weight, recommend it as perhaps the best of all eagles for the falconer's use.

THE EAGLES USED BY RUSSIAN FALCONERS.

AFTER noticing in the last chapter the antiquity of the practice of employing Eagles for the chase, I alluded particularly to the bird used for that purpose by the natives of Tartary and the Kirghis Steppes, and which is called in Russian *berkute*, and in Persian *bargut*. T. W. Atkinson, who saw this Eagle flown at deer by the Kirghis while on a visit to the Sultan Baspasihan, and heard its native name pronounced by them, spells it phonetically *bearcoote*, though this is doubtless incorrect, as well as suggestive of a false etymology, for it can have nothing to do with the bear, which is only found in the forests and amongst hill-jungle, and is never flown at by any of the tribes which train this Eagle. The Russian mode of spelling the name, *i.e.*, *berkute*, is probably more correct, and this I have on the authority of a Russian falconer and correspondent, who has also seen the bird used, and has himself kept one. He has favoured me with some very interesting remarks on the subject, to which I shall presently refer. But first let us see what Atkinson has to say about his *bearcoote*, which he describes as a "large black eagle." *

He was then in Chinese Tartary, in the country of the ancient Sungarians previous to their being conquered by the Chinese Emperor Kien Lung about the middle of the eighteenth century, and was daily expecting to meet with some of the descendants of these men. He had arrived at the yourt, or camp, of the Sultan Baspasihan, near to whose sleeping place stood a *Bearcoote* (a large black eagle) and a falcon, chained to their perches, and he perceived that every person entering the yourt kept at a respectful distance from the feathered monarch.

Elsewhere he says, "Both these birds are used in hunting by the Kirghis; the hawk for pheasants and other feathered game, the *Bearcoote* for foxes, deer, and wolves." † Near the door sat eight or ten Kirghis watching his proceedings with interest.

The Sultan being friendly, agreed to accompany him a day's journey in the direction he intended to travel, and they were also to have a hunt with the *Bearcoote*, that he might see the sport, for they expected to find plenty of game on the way. He thus graphically describes what followed:

Soon after daybreak (he says, p. 492) we were all up, and making preparations for our departure. Horses were standing ready saddled, and everything indicated a busy scene. I saw two

---

* "Oriental and Western Siberia: a Narrative of Seven Years' Explorations and Adventures in Siberia, Mongolia, the Kirghis Steppes, Chinese Tartary, and part of Central Asia," 1858, p. 487.

† "Travels in the Regions of the Upper and Lower Amoor, and the Russian acquisitions on the confines of India and China," 1860, p. 58.

Kirghis occupied with the *Bearcoote* and the falcon. Having finished our morning meal, horses were brought for the Sultan and myself. I was to be mounted to-day on one of his best steeds, a fine dark grey that stood champing my English bit, which he did not appear to relish. All my party were mounted on the Sultan's horses; ours had been sent on to the *âoul*, with a party of his people, and three of my Kalmucks. When mounted, I had time to examine the party. The Sultan and his two sons rode beautiful animals. The eldest boy carried the falcon which was to fly at the feathered game; a well-mounted Kirghis held the *Bearcoote*, chained to a perch, which was secured into a socket on his saddle. The Eagle had shackles [jesses and leash] and a hood, and was perfectly quiet; he was under the charge of two men. Near to the Sultan were his three hunters, or guards, with their rifles, and around us were a band of about twenty Kirghis in their bright-coloured kalats. More than half the number were a wild-looking group whom people would rather behold at a distance than come in contact with. We began our march, going nearly due east, the Sultan's three hunters leading the van, followed by his highness and myself; his two sons and the Eagle bearers immediately behind us, with two of my men in close attendancc. A ride of about two hours brought us to the bank of a stagnant river, fringed with reeds and bushes, where the Sultan expected that we should find game. We had not ridden far when we discovered traces of the wild boar, large plots having recently been ploughed up. This gave us hopes of sport. Our rifles were unslung, and we spread out our party to beat the ground.

We had not gone far when several large deer rushed past a jutting point of the reeds and bounded over the plain, about 300 yards from us. In an instant the *Bearcoote* was unhooded, and his shackles (*i.e.*, the leash) removed, when he sprang from his perch, and soared up into the air. I watched him ascend as he wheeled round, and was under the impression that he had not seen the animals; but in this I was mistaken. He had now risen to a considerable height, and seemed to poise himself for about a minute. After this he gave two or three flaps with his wings, and swooped off in a straight line towards his prey. I could not perceive that his wings moved, but he went at a fearful speed. There was a shout, and away went his keepers at full gallop, followed by many others.

I gave my horse his head and a touch of the whip; in a few minutes he carried me to the front, and I was riding neck-and-neck with one of the keepers. When we were about 200 yards off, the *Bearcoote* struck his prey. The deer gave a bound forward, and fell. The *Bearcoote* had struck one talon into his neck, the other into his back, and with his beak was tearing out the animal's liver. [*See* the illustration on p. 193.]

The Kirghis sprang from his horse, slipped the hood over the Eagle's head and shackles upon his legs [that is, he attached the leash to the jesses], and removed him from his prey without difficulty. The keeper mounted his horse, his assistant placed the *Bearcoote* on his perch, and he was ready for another flight. No dogs are taken out when hunting with the Eagle; they would be destroyed to a certainty; indeed, the Kirghis assert that he will attack and kill the wolf. Foxes are hunted in this way, and many are killed. The wild goat and the lesser kinds of deer are also taken in considerable numbers. We had not gone far before a herd of small antelopes were seen feeding on the plain [probably the Saiga Antelope]. Again the bird soared up in circles as before—this time, I thought, to a greater elevation—and again he made the fatal swoop at his intended victim, and the animal was dead before we reached him. The *Bearcoote* is unerring in his flight; unless the animal pursued can escape into holes in the rocks, as the fox does sometimes, death is his certain doom.

Trained eagles have long been familiar to Russian falconers, who have imported them *viâ* Orenburg from the Kirghis, and also from the Baschkyrs.

The Russian correspondent to whom I have above referred, namely, the late Mr. Constantine Haller, President of the Russian Falconry Club at St. Petersburg, sent me a most interesting account in French of the eagles used for falconry in Russia at the present day, and as this is by far the most modern account which has been written by anyone understanding the subject, his remarks are well worth publication. I accordingly translate from his letter as follows:

The Russian name for eagle is *Oriol*. The species used for hawking in Russia, and chiefly by the Kirghis and Baschkyrs, are generally *Aquila nobilis* (called *Berkute*) and *A. chrysaetus* (called *kholsann*), the most esteemed being the *Berkute;* but other species are used, such as *Aquila orientalis, glitschkii, bifasciata, amurensis, imperialis*, &c.

For the proper identification of these eagles it is here desirable to state that (1) *A. nobilis* of Pallas (Zoographia, i. p. 338) is now generally regarded by ornithologists as merely a variety of the Golden Eagle, *A. chrysaetus*, notwithstanding that the Russian falconers regard them as distinct and give them different names, *Berkute* and *Kholsann*. (2) *Aquila orientalis* of Cabanis (*Journ. für Orn.*, 1854, p. 369) is the bird to which the older name of *Aquila mogilnik* applies, bestowed by Gmelin in 1770. It is the "Russian Eagle" of Latham (Gen. Synopsis, i., p. 43, 1781). (3) *Aquila glitschkii* I do not know. It is not mentioned in Sharpe's "Catalogue of the Accipitres," 1874, nor in Gurney's "List of the Diurnal Birds of Prey," 1884. (4) *Aquila bifasciata*, it is presumed, is the bird figured under that name by Gray and Hardwicke in the "Illustrations of Indian Zoology" (vol. i., pl. 17). If so, it is identified by Mr. Sharpe with *A. mogilnik*, which inhabits south-eastern Europe, north-western India, and the Himalayas, extending into eastern Siberia.

(5) *Aquila amurensis*, Swinhoe, is again a synonym for Latham's Russian Eagle (*Aquila mogilnik*, Gmelin) showing, as so frequently happens,

Golden Eagle and Roe-Deer.

that the same species in different phases of plumage has been described under different names.

(6) *Aquila imperialis* is, of course, the Imperial Eagle, to which the older name *heliaca* of Savigny (Descrip. Egypte. 1809, p. 459, pl. 12) is now usually applied, Savigny having so named it three years before Bechstein bestowed the name *imperialis* (Taschenb. Vög. Deutschl. 1812, vol. iii., p. 553). With this explanation by way of parenthesis, I proceed with my translation of Mr. Haller's letter:—

The female *Berkute* is more esteemed than the male, especially when it happens to be a fine large one. It is, as you know, met with in many countries, and nests in Baschkyrie more commonly than anywhere else, about the great gorge of Preobragensky, near the villages of Temiassowo and Kougartschi, in the gorges of Kaguinsky and Bieloretzky.

I am told that the Kirghis also train the white-tailed eagle (*Haliaetus albicillus*) and the white-crowned eagle (*H. leucoryphus*), called by them *Kara-kush* and *Kouiruk*, but I have not personally seen these birds in their hands. Again, I have been several times assured that they sometimes have white *Berkutes*, as rarities, though I have never been able to procure one. Naturally, these white ones are the most costly. The price of a *Berkute* varies from 5 (for a nestling) to 100 and even 150 roubles, but the last-mentioned sum is the cost of a bird well trained to kill wolves, the sport most esteemed by their owners.

The flights for which the Kirghis make use of the *Berkute* are at the wolf, fox, Saiga antelope, hare, and sometimes also the bustard. Killing foxes with a trained eagle is a lucrative business on account of the value of the skins, and many a Kirghis family is maintained during a whole winter on the proceeds furnished by a single *Berkute*.

I have found from experience that the *berkute* (*Aquila nobilis*) is a bird of considerable merit for flights in an open flat country, although it has the disadvantage of being heavy to carry, and requires some precaution in managing it properly. To remedy the former defect, it is very rarely carried on the fist, but generally on a crutch of bent wood resting against a girdle, and supported by a leather strap over the left shoulder, or else it sits upon a perch made of iron, and covered with skin or cloth, which fits into a socket on the pommel of the saddle, and is thus carried on horseback. It is always kept hooded, and, after being flown, is hooded upon the quarry, or on the lure; otherwise it might leave the one or the other to attack a spectator, a *contretemps* which occasionally happens.

An Eagle is rendered docile by a course of treatment adapted to its natural disposition and habits. As its power of fasting is considerable, it is sometimes necessary to keep it fasting in order to make it keen and eager to kill something. It has to be carried a good deal, and (if fierce) "watched;" that is, kept awake at night by being set upon a horizontal swinging perch kept in motion by pulling a cord. It is "enseamed" (*essimé*) by means of washed meat (*par moyen de viande trempé dans l'eau*), and it is trained as soon as it shows a readiness to follow its owner. This is done by means of a lure made of sheepskin (or a wolf or fox skin), on which is tied some raw meat, and dragged along the ground at a little distance, which is gradually increased. The bird is then entered at a hare, or cat if intended to fly at foxes, or at a dog if meant to kill wolves, and eventually is flown loose at hare, fox, or wolf, as the case may be.

It should be remembered that, as an Eagle can fast for three or four days without inconvenience, it is sometimes necessary to let it fast for a week before finally putting it to the proof, when, if it behaves well, it is allowed a gorge. It gradually becomes more docile and familiar every day, and then requires less severe treatment. It should be lured to the ground with a skin of some kind drawn along by a cord. The Kirghis sometimes lure their Eagles with a ball of horse-skin stuffed with straw, and fastened to the saddle. They throw this out on the ground, jerking the line from time to time to keep it in motion. In my own practice I have got Eagles to come to the fist without a lure of any kind, but, in order to do this without danger, one must have confidence in one's bird, and, above all, reward it with a mouthful every time it comes back. Generally speaking, the *Berkute* is very tractable and intelligent, recognising its owner, even in a crowd.

When flown at a hare or fox, on being cast off (*étant jetté*) it rises to a pretty fair height and then comes down plump upon it, and in the event of a miss again takes wing to pursue it. The strength with which it holds and grips its prey is prodigious; its eyes seem to shine, and it looks fiercer and fiercer as its owner approaches it.

It sometimes happens that, if its stoop be true, it will split the skull of a fox at one blow, and its strength is such that it can easily knock over a young wolf, or a sheep. Even a Kirghis in the saddle (so the natives say) cannot resist it if it comes at him on the wing. This unfortunately happens sometimes if the Eagle misses its prey.

To fly at a wolf the largest and strongest bird is selected. It stoops again and again at the beast, eventually seizing it by the head and neck. Occasionally the wolf contrives to shake off the bird with a frantic effort, or by rolling on the ground; but, if he has a good start and goes away full speed, the falconer follows on horseback and helps his bird to kill the quarry.

Personally I do not think much of Eagles, and only use them myself for flying at bagged quarry, such as hares and foxes, there being little game in the neighbourhood of St. Petersburg, and the country not suitable for such flights as are really practicable only on the Steppes.

On my return from Baschkyrie I brought home a trained *Berkute*, and have had several eyesses and birds of the year, which I tamed and trained without much trouble, especially the eyesses.

To conclude, as you may be curious to know what I have at present in my hawkhouse (April, 1888), I may inform you that I have one *Berkute* that has thrice moulted, trained for hares and foxes; one *Aquila leucorypha*, twice moulted, received as a present from a friend at Narwa; one *Aquila bonellii*, which I am trying to train; three Goshawks, a male and two females, one of which has moulted six times; three Sakers, two males and a female; two Lanners (Alphanets), male and female; and seven Peregrines, namely, five falcons and two tiercels.

The remainder of this interesting letter relates to the proposed translation from the Russian of my correspondent's work on Falconry, the only one, so far as I know, which has appeared in that language in modern times.

THE BERKUTE OF TURKESTAN.

In the last chapter I referred to the Eagle which is used by the Kirghis and Baschkyris for taking antelopes, foxes, and even wolves, the name for which has been variously spelled *berkute* or *bearcoote*. In Russia, where the bird has been introduced (*viâ* Orenburg) from the Kirghis, the former mode of spelling is adopted—Atkinson, who saw this bird flown in Chinese Tartary, being responsible for the latter, which is no doubt phonetic.

In response to my request for enlightenment as to the correct orthography of this word and its signification, I received an interesting and instructive letter on the subject from an English falconer in India, Capt. D. C. Phillott, of the 3rd Punjab Cavalry, quartered at Dera Ismail Khan. He says " the spelling in old Persian MSS. is *bargut* and *bargud*, the *a* being pronounced as *u* in the word *but*, and the *u* as in *full*. In Eastern Turki (the language of Eastern Turkistan, Kashgar, and Yarkand), the spelling is *birgut*, the *i* being pronounced as in *his*, and the *u* like *oo*, as in *boot*. Before the introduction of the Arabic, the Turkis had a written character of their own, in which the vowel system differed from that of the Arabic. This is the reason that the same word is often met with spelled in different ways. A large number of Turki words, especially the names of birds, and sporting terms have found their way into modern Persian. Even in old Persian MSS. a great many of the hawking terms are Turki. Some of these MSS. are very old." Capt. Phillott has examined a good many in different parts of the Punjab, and is of opinion that they all had a common original. He has a copy of one belonging to the Maharaja of Kashmir, which is said to have been in his family for generations; and another copy of one which has been in the possession of a Rajput family of Delhi since the time of Jehangir, the son of Akbar. His own head falconer, whose father was in the service of Ranghit Singh, had a similar MS. written in Punjabi, which proved to be a translation from the Persian.

On the Nepal border, near Nepal Gamj, Capt. Phillott came across an Oudh falconer with a freshly caught Goshawk. This man told him that he was in the service of one of the many rajahs of that part, and that his family had been falconers, as he said, "from always." He added that he was the only one left in the whole district, as falconers could no longer find employment. He produced a *baz-nama* (as all MSS. on falconry are called), a portion of which, relating to the Goshawk, was written in pure Hindi (in fact, it was more Sanskrit than Hindi), the remainder being evidently a translation from the Persian.

In the preface to a third *baz-nama* in the possession of Capt. Phillott, it is stated that Jamshed (a prehistoric king of Persia) was the first man to train hawks and leopards. He is said to have given them the names they now bear, and to have caused a treatise to be written on hawking and hunting.* Subsequent kings are said to have added to this treatise, and to have obtained some of their information from Greek sources. This shows what a thorough Persian element there is throughout the literature of falconry in India, and accounts for the application, in other Eastern countries of such Persian names as *bargut*, which is bestowed upon the Golden Eagle.

In a sketch of the Turki language, in the "Journal of the Asiatic Society," Dr. J. Scully (late Medical Officer Kashgar Agency) deals in an appendix with the Turki names for birds and plants, showing that *birgut* and *kara-kush* are both names for the Golden Eagle (*Aquila chrysaetus*); *kara* signifying black, and *kush* a bird. Why, it may be asked, should the Golden Eagle be termed "black?" The name is appropriate to it in the immature stage, when the plumage is of a very dark umber brown, looking black at a little distance. For this reason Linnæus describes the species under the name *fulvus;* Gmelin termed it *niger;* and our English naturalist, Pennant, in his "British Zoology," calls it the Black Eagle. Thus the Turki name for the bird, *kara kush*, is explained.

---

* An Arabic writer, Sid Mohamed el Mangali, of whose treatise on hunting and hawking I have given some account in my "Essays on Sport" (pp. 362-370), also asserts that the art of falconry was first introduced by a king of Persia.

Capt. Phillott informs me that in a modern Persian work on falconry, by a governor of one of the Persian provinces (a brother of his late Majesty the Shah), *kara-kush* is the word used for any Eagle; *kush* being applied only to large birds, and *kush-chi* signifies a falconer. He does not think that Eagles are ever trained in India for hawking, although he was informed by an old retired risaldar-major of the 15th Bengal Cavalry, that a Kabuli falconer, who was in the service of one of the Dera nawabs, once trained a Bonelli's Eagle, and flew it at a ravine deer, which it caught, and that he took it back with him to Kabul. A figure of a trained Eagle of this species is given on a preceding page.

In Col. T. E. Gordon's very entertaining book, "The Roof of the World," a narrative of a journey over the high plateau of Tibet to the Russian frontier and the Oxus sources on Pamir (1876), an account is given by one of the party, Capt. (now Col.) John Biddulph, of the sport which he witnessed with trained Eagles (which he calls *burgoot*, and identifies with the *bearcoot* of Atkinson) while on the march from Kashgar to Maralbashi (about 120 miles), he being the first European traveller in that direction.

From Maralbashi (he says, p. 78) I went to Charwagh, a village of about 250 inhabitants, fourteen miles on the Aksir road. . . . I had good sport shooting gazelles and pheasants which abounded, and I also saw the *burgoots*, or trained Eagles, kill gazelles and foxes. I was not fortunate enough to see them kill a wolf, though they were twice flown; but the animals on both occasions being in thick bush jungle, and at a great distance, the birds did not sight them. Their owners, however, spoke of it as an ordinary occurrence.

When the jungle is not too high, they sight their prey at a great distance, and sweep up to it without any apparent effort, however fast it may be going. Turning suddenly when over its head, they strike it with unerring aim. If a fox, they grasp its throat with their powerful talons, and seize it round the muzzle with the other foot, keeping the jaws closed with an iron grip, so that the animal is powerless. (A sketch of this forms a vignette p. 88). From the great ease with which an Eagle disposes of a full-grown fox, I could see that a wolf would have no better chance. Gazelles are seized in the same way, except those with horns, in which case the Eagle first fastens on to the loins of the animal, and, watching his opportunity, transfers his grasp to the throat, avoiding the horns. The *Burgoot*, however, is not very easy to manage, and requires the whole of one man's care. Its dash and courage are great, but if flown unsuccessfully once or twice, it will often sulk for the rest of the day. When it kills it is always allowed to tear at its game for a little time; the men told me that if prevented doing so while its blood was up, it would very probably attack our horses.

The *Berkute* is even flown at the Wild boar :—

During the envoy's tour in the Artush district at the end of February (says Col. Gordon, p. 85), the villagers at one place assembled to show this sport. They were mounted on the strong, active little horses of the country, and carried clubs bent at the end like hockey sticks, with which they strike the animal on the head till he is stunned, when the death blow is generally given with some other weapon. As we in India when hog hunting ride for "first spear," so do these sportsmen ride for "first club." The trained eagle is used in this sport. It is flown at the hog on the first favourable opportunity, and generally succeeds by its sharp and powerful attack in bringing it to bay, when the men close in with their clubs. On the occasion alluded to a splendid tusker was killed in this manner. But from all I heard, I should say that the wild boar of these parts is not equal in fighting spirit to his brother of Bengal.

[A full-page illustration accompanies this account (p. 78), representing two mounted falconers and one on foot, all three carrying hooded Eagles. The plate is lettered "The trained hunting Burgut—Golden Eagle—of Eastern Turkestan."]

Of two of these birds sent with a collection to India, it was fortunate, says Col. Gordon, that one reached its destination alive to confirm his report of Eagles being trained for hawking; for his sketches of the scenes in which these birds figured were sometimes regarded suspiciously, as, indeed, was

FIG. 31.—BERKUTE AND STAG.
Drawn by Joseph Wolf for Atkinson's "Travels," 1858.

Atkinson's description of the sport when first published some twenty years previously.

Although Eagles will kill hinds and roe-deer, it is questionable whether any Eagle would attack a stag, for fear of being swept off and disabled by the antlers.

REMARKABLE FLIGHTS BY FALCONS.

FROM the days of the Roman Augurs, who professed to foretell the issue of impending conflicts by watching the aerial motions of birds, the subject of flight, for different reasons, has continued to attract the attention of observers in all ages. The naturalist, the pigeon fancier, the shooter of driven grouse, the falconer, and the experimentalist have all something to tell us about the speed of birds on the wing, and the several estimates which they have formed of the rate at which birds travel.

There can be no doubt that since the British Association in 1879 appointed a committee for the purpose of collecting statistics at the lighthouses and lightships (which statistics have since been printed in the shape of nine annual reports) we know a great deal more about the migrations of birds than could possibly have been ascertained in any other way. The time of their arrival on our shores, the lines they take on passage, the direction of the wind, and the condition of the weather which affects them, and the numbers in which they appear under these varying conditions, may now in a great measure be ascertained by reference to the reports above mentioned. But they tell us nothing about the rate of speed at which birds travel. This is a favourite subject for discussion with shooting men, and various have been the opinions expressed as to the speed of driven grouse and partridges. The opinions formed, however, are mere estimates, as a rule not based upon any experiments, but simply expressions of individual judgment founded upon practice in shooting fast-flying birds. They are acceptable in proportion to the experience and skill of the shooter, but at the best are mere guesses.

The experiments made by Mr. Griffith, as detailed in *The Field* of Feb. 19, 1887, are more to the purpose, since we get from them a record by chronograph of the time occupied by pheasants and partridges in flying measured distances, the only drawback being that the birds were not flying altogether under natural conditions, but were liberated from captivity.

There can be no doubt that when a pheasant is made to fly down a long gallery purposely constructed, even though striving towards the light at the further end, its flight must be unavoidably retarded by the feeling of confinement engendered by the bird's inability to deviate to the right or left at will. It is curious, however, that in this case as soon as the birds were *outside* the gallery, their flight across the fields, as taken by a stop watch, was slower than it proved to be *inside.*

Those who, like Mr. Tegetmeier, have turned their attention to homing pigeons, and have taken pains to ascertain the exact time occupied by these birds in flying known distances, doubtless bring us nearer to the truth. But here again a difficulty arises from the fact that the pigeons do not always fly straight from point to point, but, on being liberated, continue to circle round, sometimes for several minutes, before deciding upon their course and going away. It follows that the time occupied in flying between two given points must be less by so many minutes than the time which elapses between the moment of liberation and the moment of reaching destination, and this usually is not taken into account. Nevertheless, we get an approximate estimate of the speed of a homing pigeon, which appears to be about 36 miles an hour.*

That driven partridges and driven grouse fly much faster than pigeons must have been remarked by everyone who has had any experience of game shooting. Most sportsmen who have tried to hit them will aver that a driven grouse coming down wind is about the fastest bird that flies; but those who, like the writer, have seen a trained falcon overtake with ease and knock down a fast flying pigeon or an old cock grouse going at his best pace, know well how infinitely superior is the falcon's flight to that of the other birds named.

If we except homing pigeons, perhaps no birds afford better opportunities for estimating the rate at which they fly than trained hawks. We have only to time them with a stop-watch between some particular landmark as they pass it and the spot where the quarry is struck down, and then measure the

* See *The Field*, Jan. 22, 1897.

distance in a straight line. Falconers, if they think of it, should be able to supply some interesting statistics on this head.

Some curious stories are on record concerning the distance to which trained hawks have flown, and the time within which they have accomplished it. Some of them appear to be well authenticated.

De Thou in his famous Latin poem on hawking, "Hieracosophiou" (lib. II., xviii., p. 88), relates that a Falcon belonging to Francis I. was flown in the month of March at a Crane at Villers-Cotterets, and mounting to a great height, was carried away before the wind, and was found the following day on the battlements of the Tower of London. Henry VIII., to whom the wanderer was taken, recognising the arms of France on the "varvels," returned it to the French king, with a message to the effect that he regarded the incident "*comme le présage d'une heureuse alliance et un gage de constant amitié.*"

Conrad Heresbach, in his treatise "De Re Rustica," 1570, relates that William, Duke of Cleves, had a hawk which, in one day, made a flight out of Westphalia into Prussia. A celebrated French falconer, Charles d'Arcussia de Capre, Seigneur d'Esparron, has left on record (1607) a remarkable flight by a male Saker belonging to Henri II. of France, which was flown at Fontainebleau, at a Little Bustard (*Cannepetière*), about ten o'clock in the morning, and was taken up the following afternoon at half-past four at Malta, as the king was informed by the *grand maître*, who sent the bird back to him. ("Fauconnerie," 5e partie, chap. xxii., and "Conférence des Fauconniers," 8e journée.) The distance traversed was said to be 1500 Italian miles, and the time within which it was accomplished (according to our author) was about twelve hours, allowing seven or eight hours for rest, which must be understood to mean exclusive of the night-time, since hawks do not travel at night. But in the first place there is an error in computation of the distance flown. The journey from Paris to Malta in a straight line is about 1110 English, or 940 Italian miles (an Italian mile being equal to 1·1508 English.) If D'Arcussia's estimate of the time occupied in flying be accepted (twelve hours), then the rate of speed would be ninety-two and a half miles per hour. But the bird might well have flown eighteen and a half hours, thus: flying from 10 a.m to 5 p.m. (seven hours), resting from 5 p.m. to 5 a.m. (twelve hours), and flying again from 5 a.m. to 4.30 p.m. (eleven and a half hours); then 1110 miles in eighteen and a half hours would be at the rate of about sixty miles an hour. D'Arcussia, himself an experienced falconer, saw no reason (even at the higher rate of speed) to doubt the story, which he averred was well known to many noblemen at court, and had been handed down from father to son in successive generations of falconers. The same author mentions a hawk of his own which was lost in Languedoc, twenty leagues from home, but which returned to his house (Advis. xii.); and another which, on being flown about a league from Paris, took to the soar, and the same day was captured at Cleves, in Germany, and was brought back to Monseigneur de Guise to whom it belonged.

Sir Thomas Browne, a learned physician of Norwich in Charles the Second's time, wrote that upon good account a hawk in the county of Norfolk made a flight at a woodcock near thirty miles in one hour.*

John Aubrey, in his "Natural History of Wiltshire," written between 1656 and 1691, has a chapter entitled "Of Hawks and Hawking," in which, after quoting Sir Thomas Brown's *Miscellanies*, 1684, the following curious anecdote is related: "From Sir James Long of Draycot. Memorandum. Between the years 1630 and 1634 Henry Poole of Cirencester Esquire (since Sir Henry Poole, Baronet) lost a falcon flying at brook in the spring of the year about three o'clock in the afternoon: and he had a falconer in Norway at that time to take hawks for him, who discovered this falcon upon the stand from whence he was took at first, the next day in the evening. This flight must be 600 miles at least."

Borlase, in his "Natural History of Cornwall" (folio, Oxford, 1758) has the following observation: "Being at Trerice, the seat of Lord Arundel of Trerice, Aug. 25, 1738, I saw a hawk which, being overpowered by a crow, fell near a man at his labour in the field, who, perceiving the hawk quite spent, brought it into the house to a gentleman then steward to his lordship. The hawk was armed

* "Miscellany Tracts, Hawking," 1684. In Wilkin's edition of his works, vol. iv. p. 189.

as usual with silver plates (varvels) on its legs and neck, and Mr. Church (so the steward was called), perceiving an inscription engraved, quickly discovered the name of an Irish gentleman. The bird was a favourite, and the gentleman sent a servant from Ireland into Cornwall on purpose to fetch it." Unfortunately he does not state in what part of Ireland the owner resided.

Pennant, in his "Tour in Wales," 1778, describing (p. 8) the ancient seat of Tremostyn, in Flintshire, with its great gloomy hall, whose walls were hung with old militia guns, swords, and pikes; with its helmets and breastplates; with funereal achievements, and with a variety of spoils of the chase, adds: "A falcon is nailed against the upper end of the room with two bells, one on each foot. With these encumbrances it flew from its owner, a gentleman in the county of Angus, on the morning of Sept. 24, 1772, and was killed near this house on the morning of the 26th. The precise time it reached our country is not known, therefore we are uncertain whether this bird exceeded in swiftness the hawk which flew thirty miles in an hour in pursuit of a woodcock (in Norfolk), or that which made a flight out of Westphalia into Prussia in a day, instances recorded by the learned Sir Thomas Browne."

Col. Thornton, who died in 1823, has described a flight at a Kite near Elveden Gap, which took him six miles. He flew two Jers, Javelin and Icelander-kin, and a famous falcon named Crocus ("Sporting Tour," p. 37, note). In the same volume he has given an animated accouut of some flights at snipe (p. 143), concluding thus ; " We minuted them very accurately both times when they took the air, and the last flight was eleven minutes, during which time, moderately speaking, they could not fly less than nine miles, besides an infinite number of buckles or turns."

FIG. 32.—A FALCON IN FLIGHT.
By G. E. Lodge.

The late Mr. A. E. Knox, in his "Gamebirds and Wildfowl" (1850), relates that, when woodcock hawking in Rossmore Park, co. Monaghan, with the Hon. R. Westenra, "a woodcock, after a short chase, took the air, closely pursued by the falcon—the property of the latter gentleman—which had her bells and varvels on, with the name and address of the owner engraved upon them. In a short time both birds had attained such an elevation that they were with difficulty kept in view. At last, just as they had become like specks in the sky, they were observed to pass rapidly towards the north-east, under the influence of a strong south-west wind, and were soon completely out of sight. Some days elapsed without any tidings of the truant falcon; but, before the week had expired, a parcel arrived at Rossmore Park, accompanied by a letter bearing a Scotch postmark. The first contained the dead body of the falcon, the latter the closing chapter of her history from the hand of her destroyer, a farmer who resided within ten miles of Aberdeen. Upon a comparison of dates, it was found that she had been shot near Aberdeen, on the eastern coast of Scotland, within forty-eight hours after she had been flown at the woodcock, in a central part of the province of Ulster in Ireland."

It is not to be inferred from this that the hawk took forty-eight hours to fly about 340 miles, for this would be only at the rate of about seven miles an hour, a ridiculously slow pace for a falcon. Travelling down wind at the rate of only forty miles an hour, she would easily accomplish the distance in about eight and a half hours. Probably we shall be not far wrong in concluding that the speed of a falcon in full flight is at the rate of about sixty miles an hour. Major Hawkins Fisher timed a falcon which he flew at a grouse in Northumberland a measured mile in fifty-eight seconds.

THE DIETING OF TRAINED HAWKS.

WHATEVER may be thought of the merits of modern falconers as compared with their ancestors, it is impossible to pretend that they know one half as much about the dieting of their hawks.* From the ancient works on falconry we know that one of the most important mysteries connected with the craft was a knowledge of the pharmacopœia proper for use in the mews. Scores of the most elaborate prescriptions, in the composition of which a variety of extraordinary drugs and herbs played a part, are recorded by the writers, and were prescribed most solemnly for the winged patients to whom they were to be administered.

Without going so far as to believe in all these quaint remedies, or credit them with the marvellous effects ascribed to them in the books, one may fairly believe that at least a good many of the commoner prescriptions produced beneficial results. It is hardly likely that in an age when drugs were dear, practical men, like professional falconers, would have gone on using them for their charges unless

* For much that is contained in this chapter the author is indebted to Mr. E. B. Michell, who has been particularly successful in the treatment of the Merlin and Sparrowhawk.

they had learned by experience that the hawks which had been dosed for certain purposes did better than those which had not. It has become the fashion in these days to ridicule the idea of physicking such creatures as hawks, and to regard the practice as no less pernicious than the cupping and purging and blistering applied so mercilessly to human beings a hundred years ago. But unless we are mistaken, the mediæval falconers turned out a larger proportion of good hawks than we do, for the reason that they pursued a more careful and skilful course of dieting and physicking.

This art has now almost died out, and the few European falconers who still believe in physic adopt their prescriptions mostly from their *confrères* in India—the rajahs and zemindars, who still display a strong faith in drugs and nostrums of a simple kind. One of these recipes is now being received with favour in England, and seems to deserve its growing reputation. It is a pill intended to remove internal fat from the hawk's crop, and thus serve a purpose which, throughout the middle ages, was deemed essential in order to bring into flying condition a bird which had been in moult, or for any other cause kept without exercise for any length of time. The recipe for this pill has been already given (p. 55).

For the purges which are required for a similar purpose it is sufficient to have recourse to some of the simple medicines commonly employed for human beings. The "antibilious pills" of a well-known maker may be administered in halves at a time, well wrapped up in meat so that they are bolted by the hawk without noticing the taste. For the smaller hawks these delicacies may be cut up into quarters or even eighth parts, and may be administered without risk and with the best results.

When a hawk looks dull, and, being put on the wing, refuses to mount, and alights on the ground or on a tree or wall, it is worth while, on taking her up, to feel whether there is or not a hard swelling in the stomach, showing that there is an accumulation of undigested food. Such a swelling may for days pass unnoticed by a beginner, or even an experienced man who is careless, or who has never learnt to trouble about such matters, and the poor bird is accused of being good for nothing, whereas, if a small dose were given, the mischief would disappear, and the real character of the sufferer would come out in its true light. Very few trained hawks can be expected to keep their full health and vigour unimpaired, or even in anything near the condition natural to a wild one. In many cases the only chance of approximating to first-rate health is by means of artificial aids in the way of medicine.

However, the modern school is right in one maxim, viz., that too little physic is far better than too much. Prevention, also, is better than cure; and if general diet and exercise be carefully attended to, the worst evils of indigestion and biliousness may generally be avoided.

Beginning first with a mention of what is to be *excluded* from the bill of fare, one may mention, in the first place, *tainted meat.* No more false economy can be attempted than the buying of refuse meat, such as can be supplied at a low cost by the purveyors to zoological gardens or menageries. In hot weather the greatest care should be taken to ascertain exactly when any animal was killed of which it is proposed to use the flesh; and if the food, though to all appearance sound, is at all distasteful to any one of the hawks, it should be rejected at once, and not given to any others who are less fastidious. In cold weather it is a good plan to slightly warm the meat, which otherwise goes in a chilled, and therefore unnatural, condition into the hawk's crop. Many a fine strong bird, after taking a few mouthfuls of such cold stuff, may be seen shivering all over by reason of the disagreeable shock caused by taking into the body a sort of aliment that Nature never intended to be so taken.* Beef is very commonly given to trained hawks, especially Peregrines; and no doubt they are fond of it, and unless kept exclusively on such diet will thrive upon it. But no one can pretend that it much resembles the natural food. It should, therefore, be often varied by a lighter sort of food, such as rabbit or fowl, the whiteness of which meat makes a suitable change. Bullock's heart for the big hawks, and sheep's heart for the small ones is very good food, but as there is little nutriment in it, it will soon reduce the condition of the bird, and should never be continued for more than a day at a

* A good way to warm it is to put it in a small basin, and stand the latter in a larger one full of hot water. The meat is thus prevented from coming in contact with the water which would boil it.

time. Small hawks, such as the male sparrow hawk, and merlins of both sexes require the most dainty food supplied to them at least twice a day.

Nothing is so good as small birds freshly killed, and when these cannot be got, the alternative should be rump steak of the tenderest kind, scored across and across, and warmed till the chill is off, with a change to sheep's heart twice a week, and occasionally a mouse or small piece of rabbit, if they will eat it, which is not always the case. Pigeons are exceedingly bad for Merlins, being much too heating, and, strange to say, larks, which are the natural food of these little hawks, are also heating if given every day, and induce ill-temper and restlessness. Hobbies are supposed to be hardier, but it is necessary to be quite as careful with them in the matter of diet. They must be flown "sharp set" if they are to exert themselves at all, and yet will become useless unless fairly fat and strong.

With regard to the quantity of food to be allowed to hawks, it varies with the individual. Of two hawks, taken from the same nest, one will eat half as much again as the other, and be always voracious, whereas the latter will become wild and independent if her daily allowance is at all exceeded. The orthodox ration for a female Peregrine is one-third of a pound, or about one-sixth of her own weight, but it is impossible to judge by mere weight, for the weather, the amount of exercise, and the condition of the hawk at the time, must all be considered in apportioning her meals. It is the fashion to feed Peregrines only once a day, and in most cases this is right enough. But there are many Peregrines, especially eyesses, which fly far better if they are fed twice a day. Whenever there is an off day, and no hawking at game, it is advisable to feed in the morning at about eleven o'clock, or earlier if the hawk has "cast," as she should do, and seems "sharp set." By this means she is kept fat and strong, for very soon after the crop is empty it is replenished with a good meal, leaving no time for wasting of the tissues, and yet on the morrow, if she needs to be flown, she will be exceeding hungry. If the habitual time of feeding, when at home, be late in the afternoon, the hawk will not begin to be really sharp set till that time, so that by flying her at one or two o'clock you will be expecting her to be keen before her time; whereas, if the normal time is before noon, she will be extra hungry at any time after three, and sure to be obedient as well as eager after the quarry.

The working day of a trained hawk—and, for that matter, of a wild one also—begins only when she has got through the important but disagreeable process of "casting." It is possible that some readers, although sufficiently acquainted with natural history to "know a hawk from a heronshaw," are unaware what is meant by this term, or even ignorant of the fact that birds of prey invariably throw up out of their crop the undigested part of their last meal. When they are in a wild state this refuse consists of the feathers and bones of the birds or animals they have eaten, together with portions of gravel, sand, or perhaps grass picked up off the ground with the mouthfuls of meat hastily swallowed, and very often a part of the contents of the crop of the other bird which is eaten. Thus nothing is more common than to find in the pellet cast up by a Peregrine on the moors, buds of green heather, which have first been taken into the crop of a Grouse, and which, if left there, would have been digested in due course.

Captive birds of prey that get no "casting" wear a dull, dejected look, and lose even the distant semblance of health which they might have retained. To avert this in your trained hawk you must be careful about her "castings," and supply artificially that which the wild bird naturally finds unaided. No doubt, when your hawk is in full work, kills her live quarry, and is allowed to "take her pleasure" on it, she will get, in the natural course of events, an abundance of the best sort of "castings." In game hawking, even if she is not fed upon the quarry itself, she will get, if she kills more than one, a good sprinkling of feathers off the head and neck of her victims. But when the bulk of her meal is beef or sheep's heart it is a different thing. In such case special means must be adopted to induce her to take into her crop enough indigestible matter to serve as a vehicle for removing the refuse juices. Small feathers or wool, or the fur of a rabbit, will answer the purpose, and may be administered by attaching them to the mouthfuls taken by the hawk as she is fed up. This seems to be a better plan than one which is mentioned in some of the old books, of rolling fur or feathers into the form of a large pill, and cramming it bodily down the hawk's throat. But such soft materials are not all—though many good falconers seem to think so—that is required for "castings." The wild hawk swallows a quantity of bone, as may be easily proved by examining the remains of her feast on the ground. Part of this bony matter is thrown up; but part is digested, and, no doubt, contributes largely to keeping up the strength and health of the bird. A man who only exceptionally lets his hawk swallow any small bones cannot reasonably expect her to be in proper fettle. There is yet another thing, much neglected now, though formerly well understood—primeval substances are taken by wild hawks in the shape of sand, gravel, and the crumblings of rock. These things, technically termed "rangle," should, therefore, be given to trained hawks, and that pretty often. Pebbles larger than a pea are recommended by the old books for a Peregrine coming out o moult, and it seems to be an established fact that these hawks will sometimes pick up such pebbles off the ground and swallow them deliberately, with every appearance of satisfaction (see p. 33). However this may be, it is certain that Merlins which are allowed to eat their food on fine gravel, and which thus get a sprinkling of it with every mouthful they take, have a much more lively and sprightly appearance, and are keener after their quarry than those which habitually eat on turf, or on boards. When the small hawks are fed as they always should be on the fist, a pinch of fine gravel or sand may be thrown over the food they are eating, and the result produced in their condition will be much more salutary than a careless observer would believe.

Another detail of management, which was better understood—or, at all events, more carefully regarded—by the old school is the matter of "tiring." In the wild state a hawk takes her food very deliberately, as compared with a tame one. After the quarry has been killed there is the long business of plucking it, which means really a good deal of exercise for the back, neck, and legs. When that is finished, and the plucked bird is at last "broken into," there is still harder exertion in tearing of the meat, separating the joints, and breaking many of the bones, not only of the legs and wings, but also the breast-bone, ribs, and neck. A powerful and sudden wrench is required to break the thigh bone of a pigeon or partridge, and a great deal of force has to be used to tear off the ends of the pinions which are greatly relished by hawks, and always eaten unless taken away from them. Now all this tugging and wrenching gives the hawk's muscles an amount of exercise which they do not get in any other way, and if deprived of it, the condition of the bird is impaired. Trained hawks, which never get one-twentieth part of the exercise in flying that is taken by wild ones, especially require the kind of exercise known to falconers as "tiring" (see p. 33). Accordingly the books recommend that there should often be given to the hawk on her block or perch a tough, bony joint of some kind, as the leg of a rabbit, the neck of a fowl, or the two end joints of an old grouse, wild duck or other bird. At this she will pull away for several minutes contentedly enough, and glad of the relief from the monotony of doing nothing. The only difficulty is as to the times and seasons of giving these "tirings." Certainly they should not be given at the end of a big meal, for at that time the less exercise the better, for fear of interfering with the digestion, or "spoiling the crop," as it is called. It appears that the falconers of old fed their hawks in the morning, and about 4 p.m., or later in summer, gave them "tirings" on a block when they were put out to be weathered. Another essential use of "tirings" is this: when your hawk comes to the stage when she has to be carried and "manned," you will, if you are wise, always let her see food upon your fist as you take her about. At first she will not eat—perhaps not for hours or days—but as long as the food is there awaiting her she is less restless and less inclined to think that you are her enemy. After she begins to eat freely while she is carried, the tempting morsels which have been held in your hand for her delectation should be exchanged for tougher morsels—in fact, for "tirings," which will keep the hawk employed for three times as long as soft meat, besides giving her good exercise. Again, when a half-trained hawk is sitting on the screen perch awaiting her meal, and you have first to feed another hawk, or attend to some other business in the hawk room, what can be better than to give her the wing of a fowl off which all the meat has been eaten, and let her pull and tear at it till you are at leisure to feed her properly? If, while she is thus employed, you arm yourself every now and then with a small scrap of beef, and, putting it on the tip of your fingers, offer it to her as she holds up her head from her work, she will be very grateful for the attention, and will come to look out eagerly for your approach.

FIG. 33.—IN THE MEWS.
From a Photograph by Reginald Lodge.

LOST HAWKS.

TRAINED hawks are usually lost in one of three ways—by the ignorance of the trainer, by some carelessness, or in fair flight.* In the first case perhaps the owner has had too little experience in the art of falconry to get the hawk fit and obedient to the lure. She is not to be depended upon, and one fine day, instead of coming to the lure, rakes away down wind, and goes out of sight, leaving her master waving his lure to no purpose. It is to be feared that hawks lost in this way usually come to grief. A man who knows so little of falconry as to fly his hawks when they are not fit, generally also keeps them in poor condition, with ragged feathers and little flesh on their bones. The poor birds have, therefore, hard work, especially during the first few days, to get their own living. If they are of the larger kinds they usually visit farmyards, and get killed on a hen or chance pigeon, struck down unawares: if they are small hawks they go at the decoy birds of a bird-catcher, and so are

* In this chapter, as in the last, the author has to acknowledge his indebtedness to Mr. E. B. Michell, who has enabled him to present the reader with many useful reflections, the result of experience.

netted. A few perhaps, favoured by fortune, manage to pick up a good meal or two during the first few days of liberty without running into danger, and then, making flesh in the free air, with their muscles kept in good exercise, shift for themselves until the moulting time arrives, when, of course, they put on a fresh livery, and become undistinguishable either in appearance or power of flight from their wild relations.

The second cause which leads to the loss of hawks is the neglect of some of those precautions —often slight enough—by which the captive is secured. A knot badly tied, a door insecurely fastened, or perhaps not fastened at all, a rotten leash or pair of jesses, an unreliable swivel—each and all of these little defects have caused the loss of many a good hawk. And the worst of it is that in such cases the bird sometimes goes away as it were with a trap affixed to it which brings it speedily to grief. The leash, if it be carried away, will very easily catch in a branch, and even if it slips off, as it soon may, yet the jesses, joined together by the swivel, form a veritable hook by which the unfortunate truant is hung up and there left to perish. Such careless mistakes are extremely difficult to guard against; and more losses are suffered by amateurs in this way than in fair flight. When a hawk is lost in fair flight it is usually thus: the quarry after a long chace is killed in a thick, puzzling country. The wind may be loud enough to prevent the bell from being heard at any distance—in the case of a Merlin there will be no bell to hear—the night comes quickly on, and the hawk has to be left out to finish her meal by herself. A good hawk is almost certain to be left out occasionally in this way, especially if the quarry be a Grouse, Lark, or, in a high wind, a Rook. It is these hawks, well trained, well flown, and lost without any fault of the owner (except perhaps that he is not well enough mounted), which most easily, most quickly, and with the least risk of disaster, become wild. What is their history in the meantime? It is not difficult to trace. In nine out of ten cases the falconer, after going out at daybreak with his lure, and searching all round the neighbourhood where last the hawk was seen, will take her down after a few hours' walking, and no harm will be done. But it will sometimes happen that a hawk in high condition, though she sees the falconer, and may be within a few yards of him, will pay no attention to dead or even live lure. It is blood she wants, and the pride and pleasure of a hard flight; and she will wait therefore until there is a chance of this, and ignore her luckless owner. Within an hour of dawn she may have killed a rook or other bird in a place where the man happened not to be, and after eating it quietly in a secluded place may betake herself to tree or stone for perhaps the rest of the day. Every hour that she then spends alone and in liberty tends to aid her in recovering her instinct of freedom and her mistrust of man. Her roosting place for the second night may be some distance away, for she will choose her own convenient spot, provided it be within reasonable reach. Far away it is not likely to be, unless a violent gale is blowing; for trained hawks, especially those which have been well "hacked," will remain for a long time near where they strayed. A Peregrine Falcon—by no means a good flyer—was lost on the downs at Brighton; a few days later she was found on a Rook at Glynde, about eleven miles off. As a rule, the range of a lost Peregrine, for the first week at least, will not be so wide as this; and that of a lost Merlin—if the country holds many small birds—will not be much over a radius of a mile. Thus, if the owner or his man have any energy and prudence, they may guard against her coming to grief for perhaps a week. Keepers, farmers, and labourers should all be warned, and requested to bring word if the hawk be seen. In this way many a lost hawk may be recovered which the falconer probably would never find by his own exertions.

These reflections naturally lead to a consideration of the ways and means by which a lost hawk may be recovered without injury, and of the methods of snaring a wild one, should an opportunity for so doing arise. But the story is a long one, and must be reserved for another chapter.

DEVICES FOR TAKING HAWKS.

THOSE who have seen anything of the practice of falconry, and who know therefore what an enjoyable sport it is, if properly managed, must look upon the dead hawks dangling from "the keeper's tree" with mingled feelings of regret and vexation. When it is considered to what good account they might be turned, if taken alive and uninjured, it seems a great pity that they should be ruthlessly shot, and left to hang rotting at the corner of a wood.

Many keepers in killing vermin prefer a gun to a trap; it saves time and trouble, and makes no demand on their ingenuity; but apparently they do not reflect that shooting disturbs the coverts at a time of year when they should be kept as quiet as possible, and that clever trapping, while perfectly noiseless, is equally effectual, if not more so. On the other hand, those who do resort to trapping generally make use of gins, or ordinary rabbit traps, which, if they do not kill outright, frequently break a leg or otherwise injure a hawk so much as to render it quite useless for the falconer's purpose.

If a muffled gin were used, the case might be different; but even then, probably in its struggles to free itself the captive might sustain considerable damage to wing and tail feathers, which a falconer of course would be most anxious to prevent.

There are many ways of taking hawks alive. The late Mr. Lloyd, of Scandinavian renown as a sportsman and naturalist, and whom I had the pleasure of knowing, has devoted several pages in his book on the "Game Birds and Wildfowl of Sweden and Norway" (pp. 259-269) to the description of devices used in Scandinavia for the capture of birds of prey. For the most part, however, they are clumsy contrivances, more or less troublesome to make, and so similar in principle that there is little to choose between them, being modifications merely of two devices—namely, the well-known sparrow trap (substituting for bricks a light framework of wood covered with netting, with a live decoy bird inside), and the bow net with live pigeon for decoy, of which the Dutch pattern, as still used in North Brabant, is much superior to the more primitive form, of ancient date in Norway and Iceland.* It is unnecessary, therefore, to recapitulate; but the description of a few simple devices not mentioned by Lloyd for taking hawks may be of service both directly and indirectly to the tyro in falconry: *directly*, as enabling him to recover a lost hawk, or snare a wild one that he may happen to see; and *indirectly* as furnishing a hint to keepers who may be willing to make themselves useful to him, as well as to their own employers.

It may be well to state that at the present day in

* The Dutch method was described by me, with illustrations, in *The Field* of March 16, 1878, and has since been republished as a chapter in my "Essays on Sport and Natural History."

this country there are four different kinds of hawks used by falconers, two of them true falcons, long-winged and dark-eyed; the other two hawks as distinguished from falcons, short-winged and yellow-eyed. The two first referred to are the Peregrine (the female of which is always known as the falcon, and the male the tiercel) and the Merlin, the other two being the Sparrow-hawk and the Goshawk. Besides these might be named the Hobby, which is a summer visitor to this country; but its nest is somewhat difficult to procure, and the bird itself, though formerly held in some estimation by falconers, is not much valued at the present day. The Goshawk, I may add, is of sufficiently rare occurrence here to render its capture a matter of the greatest uncertainty; so much so that the few trained Goshawks which are now kept by falconers in the United Kingdom are all imported from France, Holland, or Germany.* The Kestrel, one of our commonest hawks, is not worth troubling about, for although it may be easily tamed, and trained to fly well to the lure, it is useless for the purpose of flying at other birds. So that, practically, there are only three hawks in this country that are worth looking after by falconers, the Peregrine, the Merlin, and the Sparrow-hawk. Of these it may be said that the two first-named keep mostly to the open country, moors and marshes, hill sides, and cliffs; while the Sparrow-hawk is a bird of the woodlands, coming closer to man's abode than either of the others.

---

* See page 142.

These may be caught in several ways; by disturbing them after they have killed something, and setting a trap on the spot with the recently killed prey as a bait; by using a bow-net with a live bird as a decoy; or by a self-acting snare, such as I shall presently describe. Having already detailed the method of using the bow-net in my "Essays on Sport," I will here only refer to two devices which are employed by falconers for recovering a lost hawk and sometimes a wild one, if they come upon it unexpectedly, and to the self-acting snare just mentioned. As simple a plan as can be devised is to peg down in the open, and close to the ground, one end of a long light line—a fishing line will do very well; at a short distance from the peg make an open running noose, which must be laid over a dead pigeon (or small bird for a small hawk), with its breast cut open to attract notice, the other end of the line being carried to a distant hedgerow, stone wall, shepherd's hut, or screen of some kind. A couple of the pigeon's quill feathers stuck in the ground just outside the pigeon, and sloping upwards and inwards, will cause the noose, when the line is pulled, to slip upwards while it contracts above the dead pigeon, and thus take the hawk round the legs.

Another method, known to falconers as "winding up," is, when a hawk comes in view, to fly a pigeon in a long light line, and allow the hawk to strike and kill it, which it will do if hungry; and then, while it is holding this lure on the ground, walk round it two or three times in a wide circle, holding the other end of the line in the hand. In this way the line gets wound round the hawk's legs, and, on attempting to fly, it is held fast. This plan is very effectual for recovering a hawk that has been flown to the lure, and, under favourable circumstances, will secure a wild hawk when bold with hunger. I have seen a trained falcon taken in this way on an open moor, after having been lost for a month, and some years ago I had constantly to employ this method when taking up a falcon that would come well enough to the lure after an unsuccessful flight, but had a trick of quitting it as soon as I approached to take her up. These two devices, and the bow net, answer well enough for Peregrines. The self-acting snare now to be described is better suited for Merlins, Sparrowhawks, and Kestrels if wanted.

Those who live in the country and use their eyes must have remarked the habit which hawks have when flying low across any wide, open field, or hill side, of perching for a while on the top of any bush, stake, or heap of stones that may happen to lie in their course. It was the knowledge of this habit that suggested the snare, of which an illustration is here given. To make it, cut a pliant sapling, forked, as shown in the illustration (Fig. 34). In the upright portion of it cut out a rectangular notch, with a hole drilled through its centre as at *b*; a light horizontal perch is then cut to fit into this accurately, and is kept in position as follows: A piece of thin whipcord being tied to the extremity of the other fork of the sapling as at *a*, is passed through the hole in the centre of the notch at *b*, and is then fastened with a knot to a horsehair noose, which is

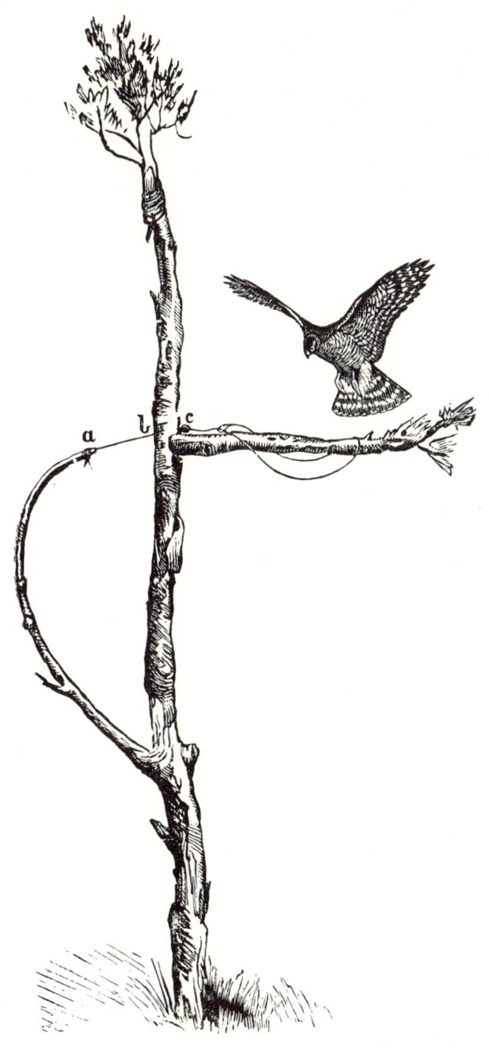

FIG. 34.—SELF-ACTING SNARE FOR MERLIN OR SPARROWHAWK.

allowed to hang across the horizontal perch, as shown in the woodcut. Care must be taken to see that the knot at *c* is not too large to pass through the hole in the centre of the notch at *b*, and also that the combined length of the whipcord and horsehair noose, when extended, is not greater than the distance between the upright fork at *c* and the extremity of the other fork (*a*) *when fully extended.*

The principle of the device is this, that so long as the tension upon the knot at *c* exerts a pressure upon the end of the perch, it sustains it in a horizontal position, but the moment a hawk alights upon it, it falls, and the noose, taking the bird by the legs, is drawn up close to the upright, against which the bird hangs uninjured until released. (See Fig. 35). This form of snare was first described by me in *The Field* of Sept. 3, 1887. It costs nothing to make, is simple in construction, and, for small hawks at all events, is thoroughly efficacious. But it must be carefully made, and the bending fork must have a good spring in it, or it will be useless. If this cannot be readily obtained, a piece of whalebone may be tied on to the upright, with a small block where it is spliced to keep it out at a proper angle. By leaving on a few leaves here and there, or tying on a sprig or two, before sticking it into the ground, it will present a more natural appearance to the passing hawk, and disarm suspicion. It is almost needless to add that the snare should be either watched from a distance when there are any hawks about, or visited as often as possible, in order that the bird may not be allowed to hang,

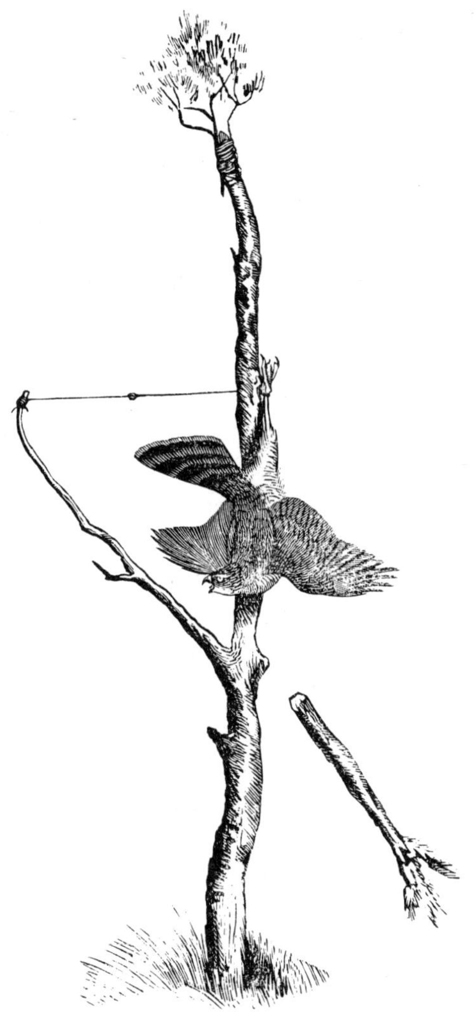

Fig. 35.—The Same Snare with Hawk Caught.

though uninjured, longer than can be helped. By a little manœuvring, a hawk may be sometimes made to fly across the open in the direction of the snare, and, if there are no trees anywhere near, will very likely perch there; but it must not be suddenly alarmed, or it will go off at too great a pace, take the air at once, and ignore the falconer's toils.

What falconers stand most in need of is a simple trap, or snare, that can be quickly made and easily transported—a device which may be used for taking a migrating hawk "on passage," an eyess as soon as it can fly, or a trained hawk that has got away, and is temporarily at liberty.

The one I have now to describe is superior to anything of the kind I have yet seen or tried. I first saw it used in Gloucestershire by my friend Major Hawkins Fisher, who has found it especially valuable for taking up hawks "at hack." To him I am indebted for all I know about it, and I will now attempt to describe it.

The various parts are few in number and easily made. Two little hoops (like croquet hoops) and a stout skewer of iron, a couple of wooden pegs to drive into the ground at either end of the trap, a small wooden "button" with a hole in the centre, a piece of india-rubber of the kind and size used for a "catapult," and a porpoise-hide bootlace; *voila tout.* The skewer has an eye at one end, through which one leg of a hoop will pass; the other end is bent almost at a right angle, to catch the lower end of the button. For bait, a dead pigeon, or the usual hawk's meat, if the bird to be caught is flying "at hack."

To set it, drive the hoops into the ground (as shown in the accompanying woodcut) at such a distance apart that a dead pigeon on the skewer will just lie between them. Beyond the hoops at each end drive in the wooden pegs; if amongst rough grass, so much the better. To one peg tie on the india-rubber, and to the other end of the india-rubber the bootlace; pass the bootlace through the button, make a knot, and carry it on, forming a simple open

Fig. 36.—Snare for a Hawk at hack.

noose over the skewer, and fasten the end to the other peg. The knot on the bootlace close up to the button must be at such a point that when the button or trigger is hooked (the upper end against the inside of the hoop, and the lower end against the turned point of the skewer), the india-rubber is stretched to double its length or more; and the length of the bootlace must be so regulated that, when the trap is sprung and the india-rubber flies back, the noose on the lace is drawn up sufficiently close to hold a hawk round the legs, and prevent its escape. The trap is simple; the art consists in setting the parts at the right distance from each other.

The way in which it is to be used will depend upon circumstances. If the hawk to be caught is "flying at hack," it has been found a good plan to cut a short, narrow piece of board, drive the hoops with sharpened ends into the wood, fixing nails beyond instead of pegs, hooking on the skewer at one hoop, but removing the indiarubber bootlace and button altogether (so long as the hawk is not wanted), and placing the board on the top of the wall or platform on which the "hack hawks" are fed daily, and putting their meat on the board for them. By this plan they get quite accustomed to the appearance of the board, feeding upon it every day, and when the time arrives for taking them up, the indiarubber noose and button are adjusted, and on the next visit the hawk is quietly and gently held round the legs.

If a "lost hawk" has to be recovered, and when found will not come down to "the lure" in the ordinary way, or allow herself to be "wound up," as already described (p. 221), the trap should be set out in the open, and baited with a dead, light-coloured pigeon, where the hawk can see it, and where, if hungry, she is almost certain to come down to it.

If the hawk be a wild one which has just been seen, not merely passing over, but flying around, she should be watched, and if seen to kill anything—a woodpigeon, partridge, or what not—she should be followed up and driven off from the "quarry," which should then be immediately placed in the trap on the very spot where killed, leaving the feathers strewn about, and a hasty retreat made out of sight. The hawk will be almost certain to return to finish her meal, and is almost equally certain to be caught.

And now, a word to the wise. To use a trap like this on ground where all hawks are ordered to be destroyed, will pay a keeper much better than shooting them, or taking them with an ordinary "gin," for he may get a sovereign for a good Peregrine falcon if her flight feathers be not broken, and will have the satisfaction at the same time of having obeyed his master's orders. But then comes the question, how is he to deal with a hawk just caught in this way? At his approach she will dash about and struggle to free herself, running great risk of breaking her feathers against the iron hoops. If he knows something about hawking, and has a spare hood in his pocket, well and good; the matter is then simple enough. If not, he should put on a glove, and approaching gently and noiselessly, kneel down and take the bird round *both* legs with the gloved hand, pull up the pegs quickly with the other hand, and lift her clear of the hoops, so that she may not strike them with her wings. She will try and bite him through the glove, but no matter; if the glove be stout he will take no harm. He should carry her gently home by the legs, and, after taking off the noose from them, hold her in the same way until some one can help him to put on the "jesses" (little light leather straps) round each leg, if he knows how. If not, a well greased strong bootlace should be cut in two, half tied round one leg, and half round the other; a knotted loop made at the end of each, a stout cord passed through these loops, and the bird pegged down on the grass in some quiet spot, out of the way of dogs or cats, to be left there with a heavy flowerpot inverted, to serve as a temporary block, until he can communicate with the falconer who wants her, taking care, of course, to feed her once a day (in the afternoon) with a dead pigeon, cut open at the breast, a thrush, a bit of rabbit, or whatever else comes handy. By this means he will lessen the risk of injuring her feathers, which would most assuredly get broken if he put her into a blackbird's cage, or a rabbit hutch, as I have known keepers to do before now.

If the hawk is not going to be fetched away, and has to be sent to a distance by rail, she should be placed in a big hamper which has been previously lined round the inside and under the lid with calico, adopting such precautions as have been already described in a previous chapter.

INDIAN SNARES FOR HAWKS.

MAJOR C. W. THOMPSON has described some ingenious methods of catching hawks as employed by native falconers in India. Small hawks such as the Sparrowhawk *(Basha* and *Besra)* and Merlin

FIG. 37. SPARROW AND LIMED TWIG.

(Turumti) are caught as follows: When one of them has been observed to come regularly to a particular tree or heap of stones, a live sparrow is pegged down in the open, at a little distance, with a short piece of

string and a nail, under an arched wand or split bamboo well smeared with bird-lime and stuck lightly in the ground, as shown in Fig. 37.

Care must be taken that the sparrow, by fluttering, cannot touch the limed twig above it, and the operator then retires to a distance as quickly as possible. The hawk sees the sparrow struggling, dashes down at it, and is immediately caught, the limed twig adhering to the breast feathers and wings, at once stopping its flight.

Another plan to catch a larger hawk, and one generally adopted to take the *Cherrug* (*i.e.*, Saker),

FIG. 38.—SNARES CARRIED BY DECOY HAWK.

is to fly a decoy hawk (such as a *Laghar*) having attached to its feet a bunch of feathers securely tied to a light piece of wood about 2in. long. This is then covered with horsehair nooses, each noose being of the strength of six horsehairs doubled and twisted. The appearance and size of this is shown in the accompanying sketch.

Each end of this bunch of feathers is covered with as many nooses as can be attached to it. The whole thing being as light as possible consistent with strength, is fastened with string to the feet of the decoy. Often at the first stoop the hawk gets entangled in some of the nooses, and then, with much screaming and fluttering, both birds come tumbling to the ground. There is yet another way in which falcons are caught in India. A quail, mynah, or parrot is used as a lure, and to its feet is attached, by a piece of cotton, a small, thin piece of bamboo about a foot in length. This is fastened at its centre to the bird's feet, and is smeared all over with bird-lime. On seeing the hawk that is wanted, the decoy bird is liberated, and the hawk, stooping at it, is sure to get entangled with the limed twig.

In the North-West Provinces the hawk catchers generally use nets. They hang a thin net between two upright rods, and peg down a live decoy bird in front of it, but not too close to it. Before the hawk can recover from the "stoop," it strikes the net, knocks it down, and is rolled up in it.*

This net, according to Capt. Phillott, is known in the Punjab as *do-gaza*. As its names implies, it is about 2 yards long; *do* means two, and *gaz* means a yard. The dimensions, however, may be considerably larger—those given below being taken from a portable net sufficiently large for all practical purposes. A fine and large-meshed net of unspun

* There is no reason why falcons should not be taken in this country by some of these methods, using suitable lures.

cotton (silk, of course, would be better) is dyed some invisible colour, such as *khâli* or black, or is simply discoloured by being washed in wood ashes and water. This net—about 6ft. in length by $4\frac{1}{2}$ft. in breadth—is suspended between two light sticks, or slender bamboos, $4\frac{1}{2}$ft. long by $1\frac{1}{4}$in. in diameter, which terminate in iron spikes about $2\frac{1}{2}$in. in length (Fig. 39). A string of the same colour as the net is threaded through each mesh along the

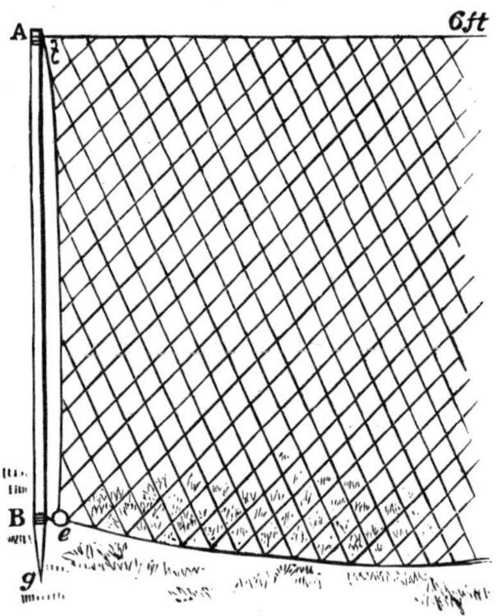

FIG. 39.—HAWK-NET.
A to B 4ft. 6in. *e*, brass ring. *f e*, cord, on which ring works.
B *g*, iron spike. Mesh at least $2\frac{1}{2}$in. square.

top, and then, together with the corner mesh, bound to the upright at A. The string is then carried on through each mesh along the breadth of the net from *f* to *e*, and finally, before being bound to the upright and finished off at B, is passed through a small brass ring *e*. The bottom corner mesh is not bound to the upright. The other end of the net is treated in precisely the same manner. It should be mentioned that the length of the net along its bottom is rather greater than along its top. A cord, in length equal to the bottom length of the net is threaded through each mesh along the bottom, and the ends fastened to the brass rings. For prevention of entanglement and convenience of carriage, the net, when not in use, is run up the cords from *e* to *f*. The uprights are then brought together, and the net, twisted like a skein of wool, is wrapped round and finished off between them.

The *modus operandi* is as follows: The snarer has observed a hawk on the ground or on a tree. He untwists the net of his *do-gaza*, slides it down the cords from *f* to *e*, plants the uprights vertically in the ground at the extreme limit of the net, and pegs down at a short distance from the centre of the net a live bird tethered by its legs to the peg. The net must be well out of reach of the decoy bird's wings, and care must be taken that the hawk's line of flight from its resting place to the bait passes through, and not over, the net. The bottom length of the net being greater than the top length, the net rests slackly on the ground, and the brass rings have no tendency to shift upwards. A handful of dust thrown over the decoy from a few yards distance will cause it to flutter and attract the hawk's attention. The hawk will then dash at it through the net. Its head and feet, and the points of the shoulders, probably get entangled ; the shock causes the net to slide a short way up the cords, while at the same time the uprights fall crossways behind the hawk, now completely enveloped. The uprights must be planted lightly in the ground. Should the uprights fail to fall when a hawk flies into the net, it may succeed in disentangling itself before it can be secured. The action of the *do-gaza* may be tested by setting it up and throwing a cap into it. The wildness of the hawk, the height at which it is perched, the amount of wind, &c., must determine the distance at which the net must be set up. *Shikras* have been taken in a *do-gaza* set up at barely 15 yards distance. Any kind of hawk may be caught in this way with the exception of the *Chargh*. If the net be set up in the bazaar in front of a butcher's shop, and a few scraps of meat thrown into the street, a Kite may sometimes be caught.

A
B
Fig. 4c.
A. B, slit.

A slightly different description of *do-gaza* is made with the uprights about 9ft. high. The bottom corners of this net are bound tightly to the upright, and the top corners are inserted into two pieces of split bamboo root—size and shape of Fig. 40—which are tied by the head to the top of the uprights. For the capture of Goshawks in the hills, three nets of this description are usually set up on three sides of a square.

In several parts of India small hawks and insect feeding birds are caught by a very simple contrivance, called a *bál-chatri* from *bal*, a hair, and *chatri*, a small umbrella. It consists of a light rough framework of split lengths of bamboo bound together in the shape of the framework of an umbrella without a handle. For approximate dimensions see Fig. 41. This framework is covered with a fine net, and upright horsehair nooses are fastened at short intervals along each rib. The bait for a hawk is a small bird tethered by the legs to a peg driven into the ground. The umbrella is then placed over the bait.

There is another contrivance for catching hawks,

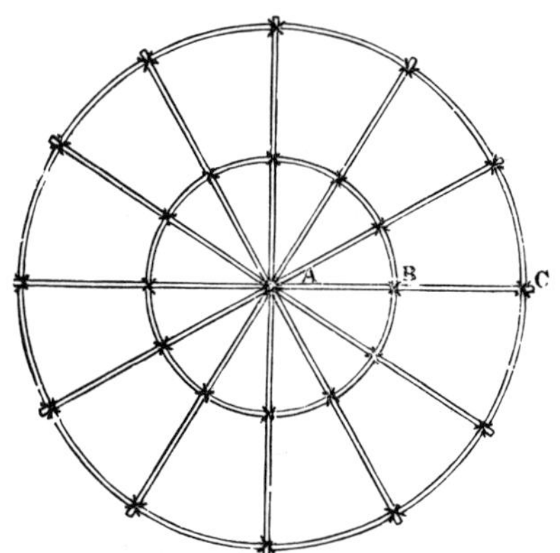

FIG. 41.—PLAN OF UMBRELLA SNARE.

A to B 8″. Depth from A to ground, 6½″. A to C 18″. Eight horsehair nooses on each rib or radius, A C. Ribs of framework about ⅓in. breadth. Horsehair nooses 2in. in diameter, made of three or more strands of hair. Mesh 1in. square.

either when on the wing or when seated, called *phande* in the south of the Panjab. A *phande* is a catgut noose (Fig. 42), about 7in. or 8in. in diameter (each noose will take a length of about 25in. of catgut), bound on to the end of a pointed strip of bamboo 6in. or 7in. long. From forty to fifty of these nooses are connected together by a line of catgut fastened to the top of each upright (Fig. 42).

The average length of the catgut between each pair of uprights is 18in. To prevent the nooses losing their shape they are, when not in use, bound by a broad tape (Hind., *niwár*) to a willow bent into the shape of the noose and its upright. These nooses are fixed perpendicularly in the ground in a circle, so that each noose slightly overlaps

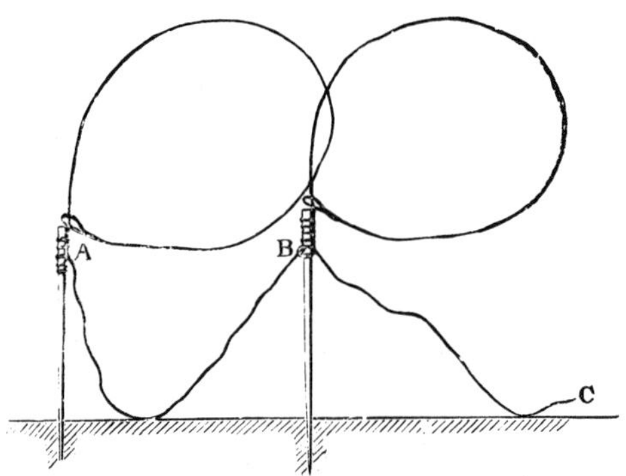

FIG. 42.—CATGUT NOOSES.

A B C. Connecting line 18″ long.

its neighbour, as in the sketch. A live bird (or field rat for a *Chargh*) is pegged down at the centre of the circle, care being taken that the diameter of the circle is greater than the expanse of the decoy bird's wings. Either large or small hawks may be snared in this manner, but for the latter the nooses should be fixed with their uprights at an angle of 45° with the ground.

THE LAW AS TO TRAINED HAWKS.

ONE of the greatest drawbacks in the practice of falconry at the present day is the risk which falconers run of having their hawks shot by thoughtless gunners. Although gamekeepers are the chief offenders in this respect, they are by no means the only persons to blame. Gentlemen who ought to know better, especially if dwelling in a neighbourhood where trained hawks are flown, are too often apt to discharge a gun hastily and without reflection at any large bird on the wing which may happen to pass within range. The result can afford but little satisfaction to the shooter who, in nine cases out of ten, does not want the bird which he has killed, while it is simply disastrous to the falconer, who thereby loses a valuable hawk for which he has given, perhaps, £3 or £4, and upon whose training he has bestowed many weeks of watchful care and attention.

The shooter may, perhaps, plead that, not being a falconer or a naturalist, he does not know a trained hawk from a wild one. But surely in these days of enlightenment, when so many books, magazines, and newspapers give information on the subject, most people must have read or heard, if they have not actually seen, that a trained hawk has attached to each leg a little leathern thong, whereby it is held on the glove while being carried. These little straps (called jesses) serve also to fasten the bird by means of a swivel and leash to its perch, or blook. In addition to the jesses—which, being six or seven inches in length, trail out behind or below the bird as it flies, according to the speed at which she is going —there is also a little brass bell attached to one leg for the purpose of indicating the whereabouts of a hawk when she has killed her quarry in roots, heather, fern, or high grass, where she cannot be seen at a distance, or when she has taken stand in some tree in covert too thick to find her immediately. This little bell, which has to be imported from Holland or Hindustan (for the art of making them is no longer practised in England), has the merit of being light and at the same time far resounding; so much so that many a straying falcon has by its means been traced and recovered. As the jesses may be seen and the bell may be heard by a gunner as soon as the bird comes within shot of him, there is no excuse for his shooting it, unless it be impetuosity of youth, or ignorance, which in the eyes of the law is, after all, no excuse. *Ignorantia legis non excusat.*

During the shooting season of 1896 two instances occurred in which trained hawks were thoughtlessly shot, to the loss and annoyance of their owners. The first case, as reported in the *Field* of Oct. 10, 1896, occurred at Bradford-on-Avon, where on

Oct. 2 the magistrates at Petty Sessions heard a summons taken out by Mr. E. C. Pinckney against Mr. Walter Pryor, for shooting, at South Wraxall, a trained hawk, belonging to the plaintiff. On Sept. 4 Mr. Pinckney was out partridge-hawking with his falconer and hawks; a covey of birds was found and flushed, and the hawk "stooped" and killed one which fell over a hedge into an adjoining field, about 150 yards from the plaintiff. While the hawk was holding the quarry on the ground, the defendant approached with a gun and shot it, to the great annoyance of the plaintiff. The bird, being well trained, was valued at £10, and witnesses were called to prove the value of trained hawks. The plaintiff insisted that, at the time the bird was shot, it was near enough to the defendant for him to hear its bell, see its jesses, and note its general tameness. For the defendant it was shown that he had the right to shoot ground game on the land on which he was, and that, seeing the hawk killing a partridge, he shot it as an enemy to game. He expressed his regret when he discovered his mistake. On the evidence adduced the magistrates did not consider there was any evidence of malice, and dismissed the summons. The plaintiff, thereupon, commenced an action in the county court, and claimed damages £10. Proceedings, however, were subsequently stayed on the defendant paying £2 into court and tendering an apology.

The second case was reported in *The Field* of Feb. 20, 1897, and was tried in the Braintree County Court on Feb. 11 before his Honour Judge Patterson.

R

The facts were similar. Mr. J. W. Thompson, of Weathersfield, near Braintree, was out hawking, when a trained falcon belonging to him happened, while on the wing, to fly within range of Mr. S. B. Legerton, a farmer at Weathersfield, who recklessly shot it. The plaintiff considered that the tameness of the bird and the knowledge that trained hawks were kept in the defendant's neighbourhood should have deterred the defendant from shooting, and rendered him liable for damages. For the defendant it was stated that he was an owner of pigeons, and that in consequence of losing some (although he had no evidence that they were killed by hawks), he kept a lookout for hawks, and on the day in question, seeing one approaching him within shot, he fired at and killed it. Plaintiff came out of an adjoining field and accused him of shooting his trained hawk. Defendant expressed regret, and said he could not distinguish it at the distance it was from him. Plaintiff commenced an action for damages in the county court. An adjournment of the case was obtained, and subsequently it was compromised.

To sportsmen in general, and falconers in particular, the termination of these two cases was eminently unsatisfactory, since it left the law on the subject still in an unsettled condition. The lawyers engaged expressed their inability to find any reported decisions governing such cases, and it appeared to them doubtful, in view of the repeal of old statutes relating to hawks, whether a trained hawk was now protected by law, and whether damages could be recovered for its wanton or thoughtless destruction. It would have been very desirable to clear up this uncertainty, and it is to be regretted that such recent opportunities were lost.

I have been at considerable pains to discover the statutes relating to hawks, and to ascertain whether any of them are still in force. The following is the result:

Hen. III. Carta de Foresta, cap. XI.		
34 Edw. III. cap. 22.	Repealed by	7 & 8 Geo. IV. c. 27.
37 Edw. III. cap. 19.	,, ,,	(except s. 2 as to eggs.
11 Hen. VII. cap. 17.	,, ,,	1 & 2 Will. IV. c. 32.
31 Hen. VIII. cap. 12.	,, ,,	Statute Law Revision Act, 1863.
5 Eliz. cap. 21.	,, ,,	7 & 8 Geo. IV. c. 74.
33 Eliz. cap. 10	,, ,,	1 & 2 Will. IV. c. 32.
7 Jac. I. cap. 11.	,, ,,	1 & 2 Will. IV. c. 32.

According to the Forest Charter granted by King Henry III. in 1217, every man in his own woods might have eyries of hawks, sparrow-hawks, falcons and eagles. Nothing is there said as to the penalties for stealing or destroying them; owing to the youth of the King at the time and the necessity for a conciliatory policy this law was probably a mitigation of that previously in force. Under the stronger hand of Edward III. the game law once more increased in severity, and in the thirty-seventh year of his reign the stealing of a hawk was made a felony presumably punishable with death. "Whereas," runs the statute, "it was heretofore ordained," etc., "and notwithstanding this ordinance the offenders doubt [*i.e.* hesitate] but little to offend in this behalf: Wherefore it is ordained and by statute established in the present Parliament, that if anyone steal a hawk and the same carry away, not doing the ordinance aforesaid, it shall be done of him as a thief that stealeth a horse or other thing." In other words he would be hanged. The "ordinance aforesaid" passed three years previously is so simple and quaint an exposition of the duty towards one's neighbour's hawk in those days that it may be given *verbatim*. It is entitled:

"How he shall use another man's hawk that taketh it up."

Also it is ordained in this present Parliament that every person who findeth a falcon, tercelet, laner or laneret, goshawk or other hawk that is lost by their Lord that presently he bring the same to the sheriff of the county, and that the sheriff make proclamation in all the good towns in the county that he hath such a hawk in his custody: And if the Lord who lost the same or any of his people for him come to challenge it, and proveth reasonably that the same is his Lord's, let him pay for the costs and have the hawk. And if none come within four months to challenge it, that then the sheriff have the hawk, making satisfaction to him that did take it if he be a simple man; and if he be a gentleman of estate to have a hawk that then the sheriff redeliver to him the said hawk taking of him reasonable costs for the time he had it in his custody. And if any man have taken such hawk and the same conceal it from the Lord whose it was, or from his falconers, or whosoever taketh him from his Lord and thereof be attainted, shall have imprisonment of two years and yield to the Lord the price of the hawk so concealed or carried away and if not he shall the longer abide in prison.

The value of falcons and the estimation in which they were held both by their owners and those covetous of becoming so without paying the price, is significantly indicated by the above facts. These statutes, however, contained no protection for hawk's eggs, and it was reserved for Henry VII. to effect this loophole of transgression. In "an Act against taking of Fesaunts and Partridges," we read:

Also it is ordained that no manner of person, of what condition or degree he be, take or cause to be taken, be it upon his own ground or any other man's, the eggs of any falcon, goshawk, laner, or swan out of the nest upon pain of imprisonment for a year and a day and fine at the King's will, the one half thereof to the King and the other half to the owner of the ground, and that the Justices of the Peace have authority by the present Act to hear and determine such matter as well by inquisition as by information and proofs.

In another section under the same head a penalty of £10—"half to the party that will sue for the same by action of debt by examination before the Justices of the Peace and the other half to the King"—is to be inflicted on any who "purposely drive them out of their coverts," and it is further ordained,

That no man "stay them for any hurt by them done, but suffer them to pass at their liberties" under the like penalty for disobedience.

Henry VIII., with more transcendant views as to the Royal power and dignity, made the taking of *the King's* nestling falcons or the eggs a felony, it being thus enacted in the thirty-first year of his reign:

It shall be felony to take in the King's ground any egg or bird of any falcon, goshawk, or laner out of the nest; or to find or take up any faulcon, jerfaulcon, jerkin, sacer, or saceret, goshawk, laner, or laneret of the King's and having on it the King's arms and vervelles (*i.e.*, varvels, see p. 24) and do not within 12 days bring or send the same to the master of the King's hawks or to one of his falconers or to the chief of the shire.

The same enactment applies to a stealer of the King's deer, who between sunrise and sunset should enter a royal park "with his face hid, or covered with hood or visert, or painted or disguised to the intent he would not be known." The necessity of repeated legislation on the subject points to the difficulty of enforcing the law in those days of sparse population and difficult communication, and it would certainly appear to have been the aim of the Legislature to make up by the fearsomeness of their threats for the uncertainty of the criminal's apprehension and conviction. Little success seems to have rewarded Henry's increased severity, for in the fifth year of Elizabeth another "Act for the punishment of unlawful taking of fish, deer, or hawks" was passed, and the preamble thereto amusingly sets out the trouble occasioned by the lawbreakers. By this statute it is enacted that,

> Any one who "shall take away any hawk or hawks or the eggs of any of them, unlawfully . . . shall suffer imprisonment for three months and shall yield and pay to the party grieved his treble damages, and after the said three months expired shall find sufficient sureties for the space of seven years after . . . or else shall remain and continue still in prison without bail or mainprize until such time as he or they so offending shall find such sufficient sureties."

It was within the power of the party aggrieved, however, on satisfaction of his treble claim, to release the offender from the suretyship and also within the power of the justices so to do if he in open session "confesses and acknowledges his said offence and be sorry, therefore, and satisfy the party or parties aggrieved." Elizabeth's enactments seem to have been equally unavailing, for eighteen years afterwards the subject had again to be dealt with by another "Act for the preservation of Pheasants and Partridges," the preamble dolorously stating:

Whereas the game of pheasants and partridges is within these few years in manner utterly decayed and destroyed in all parts of this realm by means of such as take them with nets, snares, and other engines and devices, as well by day as by night, and also by occasion of such as do use hawking in the beginning of harvest before the young pheasants and partridges be of any bigness to the great spoil and hurt of corn and grass then standing and growing in the fields.

It is then enacted *inter alia* that:

No manner of person or persons from and after the said first day of April shall hawk or with his spaniels hunt on any ground where corn or grain shall then grow (except it be in his own), at such time as any eared or codded corn or grain shall be standing or growing upon the same, nor before such time as such corn shall be shocked, cocked, hilled, or copped: upon pain of forfeiture for every time . . . to the owner . . . forty shillings.

It was evidently hoped that constant fining would prove more effectual than imprisonment, the pocket of the Englishman of that day being, perhaps, estimated as more tender than his person. Once again, however, was hope disappointed, and we find the sapient James I. endeavouring to grapple with the difficulty with pretty much the same result, if we may judge by the confession in the preamble of a statute passed in the seventh year of his reign. Thus: "Whereas in the first session of this present Parliament, there was a good law made amongst other things for the preservation of the Game of Pheasants and Partridges which hath not yielded that good success as was by the same law hoped for and intended, through disorderly and unseasonable hawking"—and it is accordingly enacted that any person convicted of so hawking "between the First of July and the last day of August" shall be committed to the "common gaol," there to remain one month without bail unless such offender pay "for every such Pheasant or Partridge" forty shillings. The same statute introduces a startling innovation in substituting the sufficiency of *one* instead of two witnesses against poachers of pheasants with snares and dogs, and the sense of this wide departure from the common law is evidently marked by the last section, which reads "This law to continue unto the end of the First Session of the next Parliament *and no longer.*"

To-day none of the statutes here briefly reviewed remain in force, having been repealed by 7 & 8 Geo. IV. c. 27; 1 & 2 Will. IV. c. 32; and by the Statute Law Revision Act, 1863.

We have therefore to consider whether there is at the present day any law existing whereby a person who maliciously or recklessly shoots, traps, snares, or otherwise steals or destroys a trained hawk belonging to another can be made liable to him for damages, or for the value of the hawk, or both. The question is not so easily answered off-hand; for, by reason of the gradual decline of falconry as a field sport, and the consequent repeal of statutes which wholly or partially governed its practice, there seems to have been long ago a cessation of litigation on the subject, and I have not met with any reported case which furnishes an exposition of the law since the repeal of the statutes above referred to.

It remains, therefore, to consider the applicability of two comparatively recent statutes, namely, the Larceny Consolidation Act, 1861 (24 & 25 Vict., c. 96), and the Malicious Injuries Consolidation Act, 1861 (24 & 25 Vict. c. 97). Section 21 of the former statute enacts that—

> Whosoever shall steal any bird, beast, or other animal ordinarily kept in a state of confinement or for any domestic purpose not being the subject of larceny at common law, or shall wilfully kill any such bird, beast, or other animal with intent to steal the same or any part thereof, shall, on conviction thereof before a justice of the peace, at the discretion of the justice, either be committed to the common gaol or house of correction, there to be imprisoned only, or to be imprisoned and kept to hard labour for any term not exceeding six months; or else shall forfeit and pay over and above the value of the bird, beast, or other animal such sum of money, not exceeding £20, as to the justice shall seem meet.

In interpreting this section it is necessary to consider, first, what animals are "not the subject of larceny at common law," and are therefore excluded from the operation of this section; and secondly, whether, if there be no evidence of "intent to steal"—the animal being merely trapped or shot, and left upon the ground—the delinquent would be liable under the statute. It is laid down in Oke's "Handy Book of the Game Laws" (3rd edit., by Willis Bund, p. 446) that as regards birds, beasts, and other animals which are the subject of larceny at common law, being those fit for food, offences may be divided into (1) those which are punishable on indictment as for larceny at common law, (2) those which are punishable on indictment by statute, and (3) those which are punishable summarily.

Those which are punishable on indictment as for larceny at common law include—swans, if marked, or whether marked or not, if in a private river or pond; fish in a tank; pigeons, although they have free access to the open air; all domestic animals which serve for food, as swine, poultry, and the like; game in a mew or breeding place, or under hens, or otherwise reclaimed, or reduced into possession, but not when *feræ naturæ*. Those which are punishable on indictment by statute include sheep (sect. 10); and those which are punishable summarily include deer, birds of game not reclaimed, hares and conies in warrens, fish in streams, and house pigeons when not confined.

The birds, beasts, and other animals which are not the subject of larceny at common law (*i.e.*, simple larceny punishable on indictment or summarily in petty sessions), and, therefore, within the operation of the Larceny Act (sect. 21), are, according to the same authority (p. 451), bears, foxes, monkeys, apes, polecats, cats, ferrets, thrushes, singing birds in general parrots and squirrels, and others, probably kept for whim, profit, or pleasure, as badgers, *hawks*, herons, *falcons*, goats, rooks—for all these are animals *feræ naturæ*, and, although reclaimed, do not serve for the food of man. Dogs also are within this category, but the taking of them is punishable under a distinct section (sect. 18) and so are horses (by indictment, sect. 10).

From this it appears that hawks and falcons come

within the operation of the Larceny Act, sect. 21, and whosoever shall steal one, or shall wilfully kill one with intent to steal it, shall, on conviction, be liable to the penalties above stated.

Whether, before any conviction can take place, it is incumbent upon a plaintiff to prove an intent to steal, is not clear. It might be reasonably supposed that if the defendant did wilfully (that is, not accidentally, but purposely) kill a trained hawk, he would render himself liable to a conviction under this section. On this point, however, I have not been able to find any reported decision. Such an act might be held to imply malice. We have then to look into the Malicious Injuries Consolidation Act, 1861 (24 & 25 Vict. c. 97). Section 41 of this statute enacts that—

> Whosoever shall unlawfully and maliciously kill, maim, or wound any dog, bird, beast, or other animal, not being cattle but being either the subject of larceny at common law, or being ordinarily kept in a state of confinement or for any domestic purpose [*as, for example, ferrets and hawks*] shall on conviction thereof before a justice of the peace, at the discretion of the justice, either be committed to the common gaol or house of correction there to be imprisoned only, or to be imprisoned and kept to hard labour for any term not exceeding six months, or else shall forfeit and pay over and above the amount of injury done, such sum of money, not exceeding £20, as to the justice shall seem meet.

Here, again, we have to weigh the particular import of the wording of the section—"whosoever shall unlawfully and maliciously kill, maim, or wound." It will be observed that the words "with intent to steal," which occur in sect. 21 of the Larceny Act, are here omitted; so that it would suffice for a conviction if a defendant merely killed a hawk, and did not attempt to carry it away. But the question remains, what is to be understood by the term "maliciously?" Is it necessary that the plaintiff, to succeed in a prosecution for shooting or trapping a trained hawk, should prove that the defendant was actuated by malice or personal spite? Or would it suffice to show that the defendant, by reason of his residing near the plaintiff, knew, or had reason to believe or suspect, that the hawk was a trained one, and that, notwithstanding such knowledge, he wilfully killed the bird, and thereby imported malice into the act? Upon this point also we have found no reported decision.

It has been held that to shoot or trap an animal in defence of property (and every owner has a qualified property in game, "Blades *v.* Higgs," 34 L.J.C.P. 286) is not a malicious offence within this section, but is the subject of an action ("Smith *v.* Williams," 9 Times Reports, 9). This might apply in a case where a trained hawk was shot in the act of killing a partridge by the owner or occupier of the land *on which the partridge rose;* but it would be otherwise if the partridge were flushed by the owner of the hawk on land where he had a right to be in pursuit of game, and was then chased and killed on the land of an adjoining owner. The result, therefore, of killing a trained hawk unlawfully, but *bonâ fide* in defence of property, may be a civil action for damages for the loss of the hawk, but not a prosecution.

The older statutes governing such cases (as

already pointed out) have for reasons stated been long ago repealed, but it would seem that under one or other of the two Acts above mentioned, the slayer of a trained hawk is liable to be sued for damages as well as for the value of the bird.

Lord Hale has laid it down (P.C. 512) that a reclaimed hawk is the subject of larceny if known to be so reclaimed, and Blackstone, in his "Commentaries on the Laws of England" (Book II., ch. 25), expressly declares:

> My tame hawk that is pursuing his quarry in my presence, though he is at liberty to go where he pleases, is nevertheless my property; for he hath *animum revertendi.* So are my pigeons that are flying at a distance from their home (especially of the carrier kind) . . . all which remain still in my possession, and I still preserve my qualified property in them.
>
> If they stray without my knowledge, and do not return in the usual manner, it is then lawful for any stranger to take them. But (he adds) if any wild animal reclaimed hath a collar or other mark [*e.g.*, jesses or bell] put upon him, and goes and returns at his pleasure, the owner's property in him still continues, and it is not lawful for anyone else to take him. . . .
>
> In all these creatures reclaimed from the wildness of their nature the property is not absolute (as in the case of domestic animals—horses, kine, sheep, poultry, and the like), but defeasible; a property that may be destroyed if they resume their ancient wildness and are found at large. . . . But while they thus continue my qualified or defeasible property they are as much under the protection of the law as if they were absolutely and indefeasibly mine, and an action will lie against any man that detains them from me, or unlawfully destroys them.

Further on, he remarks "Yet to steal a reclaimed hawk is felony both by common law and statute." The statute, no doubt, to which he referred was 37 Edw. III. c. 19, then in force, but which was repealed, as above stated, by 7 & 8 Geo. IV. c. 27.

It is laid down in Hawkins's "Pleas of the Crown" (p. 149, ch. xix., sect. 40) no doubt following Blackstone, that it is not an offence to take and carry away an animal (*e.g.* a hawk) which, though really tame, is wandering far from its habitation as if it were wild, when it is not known to be tame by the person who takes and carries it away. But as this could not apply in the case of a dog wearing a collar with the owner's name and address engraved thereon, so in the case of a trained hawk the jesses and bell upon the legs would afford sufficient evidence of ownership to justify the view taken by Blackstone.

If, then, a man have a property in a trained hawk, it follows that if it escapes he may take it wherever he can find it. He may even take it by reasonable force from a person wrongfully detaining it ("Blades *v.* Higgs," 34 L.J.C.P. 286). As an alternative, the latter may be sued in the county court for its recovery, or value, and perhaps damages for its detention, unless he has bought it *in market overt.* The County Court Rules provide (Order XXV. r. 50) that the judge may make an order for the delivery by the defendant of specific property, or in default for payment of the value of such property (to be assessed by the judge or jury), and that under such a judgment the plaintiff may obtain a warrant for delivery, and in default the sheriff may distrain and hold the defendant's goods until the return of such property or its assessed value.

In the case of a trained hawk the owner must positively identify the bird as his own, and for this purpose he may, before the trial, obtain an order to inspect it. Moreover, he is entitled to recover it without paying anything for its keep; for, according to a decision in "Binstead *v.* Buck," the finder has no lien for its keep upon any animal thus wrongfully detained.

If a man purchase a hawk wearing jesses or other marks of ownership *in market overt*, as, for example, in Leadenhall Market, or in the shop of any dealer in live animals where such things are usually sold, he has a good title to it against everyone, including even the former possessor from whom it may have been stolen; and in that case the latter has no remedy.

Since the above considerations were penned a magisterial decision has been obtained as to the illegality of shooting a hawk which has been reclaimed and trained, and the consequent liability of the shooter for its value.

In a case lately tried (Oct. 1897) in the County Court at Trowbridge, His Honour Judge Gardiner, without alluding to the statute law, based his decision upon the common law as expounded by Blackstone.

The following report of the case appeared in *The Field* of Oct. 23, 1897:

In the Trowbridge County Court, on Oct. 15, before His Honour Judge Gardiner, Erlysman C. Pinckney, of South Wraxall, Wilts, sued Ernest Collins, of Forewood's Common, Holt, for £10 damages for shooting a trained hawk. Mr. J. Compton, of Bradford-on-Avon, appeared for the plaintiff, who, in his evidence, stated that he was partridge hawking at South Wraxall on Sept. 13, on land over which his father had sporting rights. The hawk, a female Peregrine, known in hawking parlance as a "falcon," after "waiting on," had flown and caught a partridge, and whilst coming to the ground with it had been fired at twice by the defendant who was standing in the adjoining road, the second shot breaking the hawk's wing.—His Honour: Does any other person in the immediate neighbourhood keep trained hawks?—Plaintiff: No, not nearer than fifteen miles. Plaintiff, continuing, said that defendant came to him next morning and admitted that everyone in the neighbourhood knew of his hawks. The falcon might have been known as a trained hawk from the leather straps on the legs, called "jesses," which she was wearing, and from the bell she carried, which could have been heard 250 yards away. Asked the value of the hawk, plaintiff said it cost him £3 untrained in July last, and he valued it at £10, as it was a very fast and well-trained bird.—Thomas Allen stated that he was falconer to Mr. Radclyffe, of Wareham, and had been accustomed to hawks all his life, and had been with Mr. Radclyffe eight years. He considered the hawk shot a very valuable bird, and for a good game hawk at that period of the season £10 was below its value. Mr. Radclyffe possessed a hawk for which he would not take £50. A falcon, after having its wing broken, would be utterly worthless.—John Frost, plaintiff's falconer, who was with him, corroborated the statement as to how the hawk had been shot, and said that at the second shot the hawk dropped her partridge and fell to the ground.—His Honour: What height from the ground was the hawk when the first shot was fired.—Winess: About 20ft.—His Honour: Can you swear that at the time the hawk was shot it was carrying a partridge?—Witness: Yes. Defendant admitted to him the next morning that, when he was under keeper on some adjoining land, his master, on seeing the plaintiff out with his hawks, had asked what they were doing, and that he, defendant, had replied that they were partridge hawking.—Police Inspector Reed deposed to seeing the defendant on the morning of Sept. 14, and that after cautioning him, the defendant had admitted that he shot the hawk, and that it was carrying a partridge at the time.—The defendant, in his defence, said that he was coming along the road on Sept. 13, and seeing the hawk flying across the field, put two cartridges into his gun, and fired both barrels; the hawk was 50 yards high; he did not hear a bell or see that she had a partridge. He did not know that there were any trained hawks in the neighbourhood.—His Honour: There is only one thing I want cleared up. Is there any law that protects trained hawks? In reply Mr. Compton read extracts from "Blackstone's Commentaries," showing that a qualified property subsists in animals *feræ naturæ per industriam hominis*, and that the law extended that possession further than the mere manual occupation, for a tame hawk whilst pursuing its quarry in the owner's presence, though at liberty to go where it pleases, nevertheless belongs to the owner, "for that it hath *animum revertendi*." His Honour: Yes, and I have no doubt there are other similar authorities. In summing up, he said: It has been proved to my satisfaction that the defendant Collins was aware that plaintiff kept trained hawks, and therefore, if he chooses to fire at a hawk, he must take his chance of its being a tame one. Moreover, whether by intention or accident he shot the plaintiff's hawk, the latter was the loser by it. I have had expert witnesses to prove the value of the hawk, and therefore I must give judgment for the amount claimed. There will be judgment for the plaintiff for £10, with costs of solicitor and witnesses.

It is to be hoped that the report of this decision will be far-reaching, and that, for the future, "falconers' favourites" may enjoy that immunity from molestation which is enforceable in the case of valuable sporting dogs, and equally valuable homing pigeons.

Every true sportsman should be actuated, not merely by enthusiasm for his own particular branch of sport, but by a feeling also of toleration for the sport of others.

FINIS.

INDEX.

CORRIGENDA.

Page 32, line 23, *after* "he would not feed them" *insert* "before flying on."

Page 43, line 30, *for* "bog cadge" *read* "box cadge."

Page 47, line 14, *after* "in the evening" *add* "if flown the same day."

Page 55, last line, *transpose the words* "gullet" and "crop."

Page 162, line 29, *for* "conspicuusly" *read* "conspicuously."